For decades our society has fostered a "low view" of marriage and easy divorce. With *Your Marriage Masterpiece*, Al Janssen makes a compelling case for the sacredness and permanence God intended for this unique relationship. This book will not only enlarge your vision and understanding of matrimony, but it will deepen your understanding of the incredible love of Christ. This is exactly the kind of "high view" of marriage that is needed in the church and in our culture today!

BILL MCCARTNEY
Founder & President, Promise Keepers

Just as the North Star provides vision and guidance for seamen in various circumstances, so will *Your Marriage Masterpiece* provide vision and guidance for couples to maintain their bearings as they navigate the treacherous waters of life together.

DR. TONY EVANS
Senior Pastor, Oak Cliff Bible Fellowship
President, The Urban Alternative

A book is only as great as the heart of its author. *Your Marriage Masterpiece* is a great book because it has a great author. I've known Al Janssen for several years, and he, like this insightful book, is legit. Marriage needs creativity, integrity, and all-out commitment, not just to stay together but to thrive joyously through the years! That is precisely the message of this book and the man who wrote it. This book is a first aid kit for the hurting, Gatorade for the exhausted, and the bow of William Tell for the marriage that's succeeding but wants to get to the heart of the bull's-eye.

JOE WHITE
President, Kanakuk Kamps

Your Marriage Masterpiece provides us with the most important ingredient for a successful marriage: understanding the purpose of marriage, from God's intention. What a refreshing and revitalizing message!

> MICHAEL A. ROSEBUSH, PH.D.
> Vice President of Education, Focus on the Family

Al Janssen in *Your Marriage Masterpiece* offers a unique picture of the tapestry of marriage that will inspire you to make yours go the distance.

> DAVID AND CLAUDIA ARP
> Founders of Marriage Alive Seminars and
> Authors of *10 Great Dates to Revitalize Your Marriage*

Al Janssen combines creativity and a solid grasp of biblical truths to produce a fresh perspective for married couples. Whether you're a newlywed or celebrating your 50th anniversary, experiencing a fulfilling marriage or going through a heartbreaking separation, God has an important message to share with you. It's right here in *Your Marriage Masterpiece*.

> RANDY ALCORN
> Director, Eternal Perspective Ministries
> Author of *Deadline* and *Safely Home*

Al Janssen has written a book on the Good Book that tells us how a sick marriage can heal, a good marriage can get better, and the best marriage can understand itself. No book I have read in recent years helps me understand how God feels and what the Bible has to say quite like this one.

> DR. CALVIN MILLER
> Beeson Divinity School

A foundation book for our time. No other institution is more basic to our nation than marriage. *Your Marriage Masterpiece* is a powerful, biblically based reminder of what God had in mind when He called two to become one. If you are looking for a wedding gift that will encourage a couple just starting out, or for a book that will breathe life into a marriage that needs a refresher, you've found it!

DENNIS RAINEY
Executive Director, FamilyLife

Most marriage books start and end with "how to." But Al Janssen asks a much deeper question, "Why did God create marriage?" The answer can provide each reader with the foundation for doing all those "how to's," as well as giving him or her a wonderful picture of just why marriage is so important to Almighty God. Art teachers say to their students, "Study the Masters." For those serious about having loving, lasting relationships, I say, study *Your Marriage Masterpiece*.

JOHN TRENT, PH.D.
Author, Speaker, and President, Encouraging Words

By delving into God's model for marriage in *Your Marriage Masterpiece*, Al Janssen gives a foundation for what I have been teaching all these years.

GARY SMALLEY
Author and Speaker, Founder of Smalley Relationship Center

Our longtime friend, Al Janssen, has completed a "touchdown pass" with this book, *Your Marriage Masterpiece*. We will be recommending it to couples, newly married to celebrating the golden years, who seek to go the distance in their marriages.

NORM AND BOBBE EVANS
Pro Athletes Outreach

FOCUS ON THE FAMILY

your
marriage
masterpiece

discovering
GOD'S AMAZING DESIGN
for your life together

AL JANSSEN

Tyndale House Publishers, Inc., Carol Stream, IL

ISBN-10: 1-58997-228-7
ISBN-13: 978-1-58997-228-5

A Focus on the Family book published by Tyndale House Publishers, Carol Stream, Illinois.

Focus on the Family and the accompanying logo and design are federally registered trademarks of Focus on the Family, Colorado Springs, CO 80995.

TYNDALE and Tyndale's quill logo are registered trademarks of Tyndale House Publishers, Inc.

Editors: Larry Weeden, Ray Seldomridge
Cover design by Jennifer Ghionzoli
Cover photograph copyright © by Veer. All rights reserved.
Author photograph by Reverend James Hayne. Used by permission.

Library of Congress Cataloging-in-Publication Data
Janssen, Al.
    The marriage masterpiece : a bold new vision for your marriage / by Al Janssen.
        p. cm.
Includes bibliographical references.
    ISBN 1-56179-905-X
    1. Marriage—Religious aspects—Christianity. I. Title.
    BV835.J36 2001
    248.4—dc21

                                    2001003477

Printed in the United States of America
08 09 10 11 12 13 14/10 9 8 7 6 5 4 3 2 1

To
Jo Ann
The woman God chose for me.
I love the picture He is painting in our marriage.

To
Focus on the Family
This is why we promote the institution of marriage as
"a permanent, lifelong relationship between a man and a woman,
regardless of trials, sickness, financial reverses, or
emotional stresses that may ensue."

Contents

Foreword

Earlier this week, while taking a Sabbath rest from our busy schedule, I took my wife, Barb, out on a date. Married more than 32 years, after two kids and five grandchildren, dating my wife is more fun than ever. We had a late lunch in a quaint restaurant and then stopped at an art store where Barb had worked before we were married.

A portrait artist by training, over the years Barb's artistic talents had been pushed aside by the busyness of life, the time pressures, our ministry, and the needs of those who call her wife, mother, and Gaga. But as we walked the aisles of this artist's haven, I saw something in Barb's face. As she picked out brushes, paints, and supplies, her countenance lifted. She was envisioning time in her studio bringing a portrait of our five grandchildren to life on canvas.

Like the masterpiece in Barb's vision is God's masterpiece of marriage. The Creator did indeed dream up the whole thing called marriage. He envisioned it as a way to draw us to Himself. Throughout this great country, couples are establishing beachheads that champion marriage—marriages that celebrate God's original masterpiece—and have embraced the truth that at the end of the day our marriages are not about us . . . they are about glorifying Jesus Christ. Your marriage and my marriage do matter to God, our churches, our communities, and ultimately our culture, because marriage—biblical marriage—is God's first line of defense of the gospel.

Yet for so many in our culture, a perfect storm is choking out His creation. Many are choosing the counterfeit lifestyle of cohabitation, believing it will satisfy. Others are walking away from marriage concluding that they must have made a mistake the day their marriage was entered into. And finally, others have given up altogether on the institution of marriage, believing that it is outdated and no longer effective in our time. Our flesh, our culture, and Satan—the enemies of our marriages—all conspire to destroy the masterpiece.

In the midst of this battle, Al Janssen's book *Your Marriage Masterpiece* paints the picture of God's design for marriage—marriage that honors Him and establishes a foundation upon which a husband and wife can capture His plan. Clearly, God's design is still as vibrant and foundational as it was in the Garden of Eden.

I've known Al and Jo for 20 years and they are the real deal. Al writes with passion, he draws us to the original Author of marriage, and he honors the reader by blending biblical truth, gut-level honesty and integrity, and a road map whereby we can be found faithful.

I can't wait until Barb someday pulls back the cover and shows me her masterpiece. Meanwhile, I'm thankful that you don't have to wait for Al Janssen's book, *Your Marriage Masterpiece*, because you're holding it in your hands. And like me, I'm certain you are grateful that before you were born, God had already painted a masterpiece, in His Word, of what a distinctively Christian marriage looks like.

Thank you, Al Janssen, for pulling back the cover and shining the light on *His* masterpiece of marriage.

—Dr. Gary and Barbara Rosberg—America's Family Coaches
   Coauthors of *6 Secrets to a Lasting Love, The 5 Sex Needs of Men and Women,* and *The 5 Love Needs of Men and Women*

Restoring the Masterpiece

Across the ceiling of the Sistine Chapel spans one of the greatest artistic triumphs in history. From 1508 to 1512, the artist Michelangelo lay on his back and painstakingly painted the creation, fall, and destruction of mankind by flood. One does not have to be an art expert to appreciate the genius of this creative work. Rarely has anyone so beautifully depicted the human form. Never has the scope of the divine and human drama been so powerfully portrayed.

Michelangelo's magnificent art started to fade almost immediately after he painted it. Within a century of completing his work, no one remembered what his original frescoes had really looked like. In subsequent centuries, well-intentioned restorers covered the work with a varnish in a short-lived attempt to revitalize the colors. That only served as a magnet for more smoke and dirt until, as painter Biagio Biagetti described it in 1936, "we see the colors of the Sistine ceiling as if through smoked glass."

In 1981, a scaffold was erected and plans were made to clean other artists' priceless frescoes that also adorn the chapel. At the top of the scaffold, the restorers were able to reach one of the lunettes of Michelangelo's ceiling masterpiece—a representation of Mathan and Eleazar, ancestors of Christ. For Fabrizio Mancinelli, director of restoration work in the famous chapel, this was the chance he needed to perform a critical experiment. A special solution called AB-57 was given to chief restorer Gianluigi Colalucci. Carefully the pair climbed the scaffolding. Colalucci knelt down at the bottom corner of the lunette and gently washed a minute portion of the painting with distilled water. He brushed on the mild cleaning agent, let it sit for just a moment, then removed it with a sponge dipped in distilled water.

Twenty-four hours later, the pair repeated the process. Mancinelli was pleased by the results. "We will clean the complete lunette!" he proclaimed. In the following days, Colalucci painstakingly repeated the cleaning process, covering only a square inch or two each time. After all, this was Michelangelo, and one didn't take chances with the great master!

As the two restorers proceeded, they grew increasingly excited. They invited art experts from the Vatican and throughout Italy to examine the work. When the lunette was completely cleaned, the result was a stunning display. No one had imagined that beneath centuries of grime lay such vibrant colors. This was not the Michelangelo known by art critics. That artist was the master of form, his paintings resembling sculpture more than paint on plaster. This "new" artist, never before viewed by modern eyes, was also a master of color—azure, malachite green, rose, and lavender of such nuance that one could only gaze in amazement.

The success of the first lunette emboldened the restoration team to tackle all of the lunettes on the entrance wall, and to make plans for the most ambitious restoration project in art history—the cleaning of the entire ceiling of the Sistine Chapel.

A six-yard-wide bridge was built for the project and attached in the original holes used for Michelangelo's bridge. The restoration was done inch by inch. Cleaning solutions were adjusted. For portions where Michelangelo had painted on dry plaster, a different technique was used compared to those places where he'd painted on wet plaster.

The task was completed on December 31, 1989. It had taken twice as long to clean the ceiling as the artist had needed to paint the original. But the result was breathtaking. For the first time in nearly 500 years, people viewed this masterpiece the way it was originally intended, in all of its color and beauty.

Not surprisingly, there was controversy over the restoration. Some critics protested that the process had actually destroyed the work, and that Michelangelo would pound his head in frustration if he could view it today. But most experts agreed that years of meticulous research had uncovered the true intent of the artist. It's just that no one expected the results to be so stunning.[1]

There is another artistic masterpiece that needs serious restoration work. It is the relationship called marriage, and it was designed by the greatest Artist in history.

Casual observation would lead one to conclude that the institution of marriage is not highly esteemed today. Each year millions of couples worldwide end their marriages via divorce. Movies and television programs glorify casual sex, cohabitation, gay unions—virtually any alternative to traditional marriage between one man and one woman for life. Some social observers are daring to suggest that marriage is no longer necessary or even desirable. Yet, for an institution in such supposed decline, it is striking that nine out of ten people worldwide choose to marry at least once in their lives.[2]

Most if not all of those couples begin their unions with the hope that their relationship will last for life. Sadly, many have their expectations of living "happily ever after" together dashed.

Perhaps it is time to answer the fundamental question—"Why marriage?" Why bother with the obligations, sacrifices, and even the joys of marriage? Why risk lifelong unhappiness if marriage is nothing more than a legal arrangement between two adults? Why remain in a tough marriage if there is little hope of lasting improvement?

To answer these and other questions, we need to examine what marriage looked like in its original state. How has the picture faded in the passage of time? Can we discover the Artist's original intent? Are solvents available to clean the masterpiece and restore it to its initial luster?

Let us lift the veil and explore the great Artist's work. Perhaps we can discover what our marriages should look like and how they can shine in their intended colors.

1

Whatever Happened to Happily Ever After?

Only seven months after my wedding day, my comfortable assumptions about marriage were challenged at the core.

Jim*[1] stood 6'4" tall and could throw a baseball 94 miles per hour. Yet, over the course of six years, he'd spent only four tantalizing weeks in the major leagues. The rest of his time was spent bouncing from one minor league team to another. Jim and I leaned against his Camaro and talked outside Diablo Stadium in Tempe, Arizona, where Jim had just pitched two innings in a spring training game. It hadn't gone well. Unless there was a dramatic turn of events, in about two weeks Jim would start his seventh season in the minor leagues.

In the late afternoon desert sun, we discussed his future. "Bonnie* thinks I should retire if I don't make the big club this spring," Jim said. "I simply can't do that. I can't give up when I'm this close. I'm no quitter!" Bonnie was Jim's wife, and at most games the striking blond was seen socializing in the wives' section.

"I didn't see Bonnie at the game today," I noted.

"She decided not to come. We had a big fight last night."

A few evenings earlier, my wife, Jo, and I had enjoyed dinner with the couple and learned that they had been high school sweethearts. Bonnie was a cheerleader; Jim was the star three-sport athlete who signed a lucrative contract out of high school. They'd married after his first season and quickly spent his $40,000 signing bonus.

Cautiously, I inquired about the cause of their marital discord. Jim shook his head. "The same things we've fought about for a couple of years now. Bonnie wants to settle down. She counted the number of homes we've lived in since we married. Between nine minor league towns, spring training, and our off-season home, we've moved 21 times. She wants me to get a real job, buy a house, and start a family."

Though I'd only been married for a few months, that didn't sound unreasonable to me. However, I certainly didn't feel qualified to be a marriage counselor, so I figured the best thing to do was listen.

"I can't seem to please her," Jim said. "She doesn't understand that I have to do this. I have to go as far as I can in baseball. I simply can't walk away from the game."

Of course, every athlete's career ends sooner or later—usually sooner. In my work with Pro Athletes Outreach I'd met a number of athletes who refused to recognize when it was time to move on to a new phase of life. "Have you given any thought to what you might do after baseball?" I asked.

"Of course I have! I've taken a few college classes in the off-season. But nothing really interests me. Bonnie keeps reminding me that I need to plan for the future. I know that! Why does she have to keep nagging me? She's always bugging me about money— we never have enough to satisfy her." Unspoken was his hope that he might someday exchange a paltry minor league salary for a lucrative major league contract.

Jim turned and faced me. He could be an aggressive, intimidating person. That attitude served him well on the pitcher's mound, but I could imagine this in-your-face approach might not be appreciated by his petite wife. Bonnie had already confided to my wife that she was scared of Jim, afraid that one day he might hurt her in one of his fits of anger.

"Al, I'm thinking of leaving Bonnie."

"What! Why?"

"I'm not happy." The words hung there. "God wants me to be happy, doesn't He? Since I'm not happy, then I think I should get a divorce."

"What about her feelings? You can't just leave her!"

"Why? I suppose you are going to tell me that God doesn't want me to divorce."

"Well, yes, that's true. God hates divorce." Since I'd spoken several times to the team in chapel services and Bible studies, Jim was willing to ask me hard questions. But I could tell he didn't really want to know God's views on this particular subject.

"What if I made a mistake? We got married just a year out of high school. We were young. We didn't really know what we were doing. Are you telling me I simply have to gut it out for the rest of my life? God doesn't want me to be miserable, does He?"

I stammered. "No, He doesn't. But surely you two can work things out. I know you must love each other."

"Maybe we did at one time. But now, I just don't have any feelings for Bonnie."

"Feelings come and go. You can get the feelings back!"

Jim shook his head and pulled his car keys from his pocket. "I don't know. Is it worth fighting for an unhappy marriage?"

As my friend drove away, I stood in the parking lot and mulled over his words:

"I'm not happy."

"I just don't have any feelings for Bonnie."

"God doesn't want me to be miserable, does He?"

"Is it worth fighting for an unhappy marriage?"

Something deeply troubled me. I knew statistically that many marriages failed, but this was my first confrontation with a marriage that was disintegrating before my eyes, and I didn't know what to say or do. I wasn't confident that I really understood what the Scriptures taught about this subject; my reactions were more intuitive. Both Jo's parents and my parents had been married for more than 30 years, and we believed that God had brought us together for life. Were we naïve to believe that our marriage would go the distance just because our parents' marriages did? Could we really survive against the overwhelming cultural trends of the time?

My conversation raised questions that begged for answers. If someone is not happy, why should he or she stay married? For singles confronting the risk of potential unhappiness within marriage, why get married at all?

The Culture of Self-Fulfillment

When Jo and I were married on August 6, 1977, it was "for better or worse, for richer or poorer, in sickness and health, and for as long as we both should live." At least, those were the words we repeated back to the pastor. Unspoken in those vows was the expectation that we would live happily ever after. Isn't that what every couple thinks? Of course, we soon realized that our marriage, like every marriage, has its rough spots. Every day doesn't provide a "happily ever after" experience. Still, the dream persists.

I've thought a lot about Jim and Bonnie over the years. They didn't separate that spring, and he played one more season in the minor leagues before being released. They moved back to their hometown on the East Coast, where Jim found work as a car salesman. Jo and I soon lost touch with them. A few years later, I learned through a mutual friend that Jim and Bonnie never had children, and eventually they did divorce. When I heard that news, I felt a wave of sadness. Again, I wondered what, if anything, might have made the difference for them. Must we simply accept the cultural realities that nearly 50 percent of married couples will eventually divorce?[2]

But then I wonder, if Jim and Bonnie were unhappy together, why not part company? If marriage hinders the things we seek— self-fulfillment, personal growth, spiritual wholeness—why stick it out? After all, if we marry in order to be happy, then it makes sense that many who are unhappy today opt out, doesn't it?

The experience of Jim and Bonnie is not unusual among our friends. Here are just three examples:

1. I sit in a barber chair as my hairstylist, waving scissors for effect, asks me, "God hates divorce, right?" Yes, I answer, God hates divorce. "So God must hate anyone who gets a divorce?" No, I explain, God loves all, but He hates divorce because it destroys a beautiful creation of His. Why, I probe, is she asking this question? Fighting back tears, she says she has just consulted with a divorce attorney. What should I say to her?

2. My wife talks on the phone with an out-of-state friend who cries as she says, "I've lived without hope for 14 years." Her husband is addicted to pornography. He's perceived as a "good" Christian man, active in the church. But his secret addiction has destroyed the person closest to him and their three children. The man, unable to confront his condition, buries his guilt with alcohol. He frequently comes home drunk and lashes out at anyone within reach. She is considering a separation for her safety and that of the children. Is this a marriage worth fighting to save?

10   your
m a r r i a g e
m a s t e r p i e c e

3. A longtime friend, Benjamin*, reveals that he has lived a lie for much of his adult life. He now claims he is really a homosexual. He is leaving his wife and two teenage sons, who are absolutely devastated. The older of the boys is exhibiting destructive behavior, but Benjamin is unmoved. He says he can no longer deny himself sexual fulfillment, even if his family pays a terrible price. Is he right?

Isn't it obvious in these cases that the people involved are unhappy? I wish these were unusual situations, but unfortunately I could recite many examples, and, no doubt, so can you. So why should these people remain married? And why should any young adult observing them even consider marriage?

Why Be Married If I'm Not Happy?

It should come as no surprise that many, in fact, would rather not risk such heartache. *Time* magazine ran a cover story in August 2000 on the phenomenon of many women choosing not to marry. Why? They have decided that "being on their own was simply better than the alternative—being stuck with a man, and in a marriage, that didn't feel right." Thus one woman ended a seven-year relationship because "I wasn't happy. I didn't think I could make him happy and retain my spirit, what makes me shine." Another woman ended a 10-year relationship with a man she says she loves but "is behind her in personal and professional growth."[3]

Behind such thinking is the view that marriage is disposable, entered into and exited according to an individual's needs. There is a growing sense among some that marriage is a nice thing to have if it fits your lifestyle. If not, there are alternatives. For example, writer and businessman Philip D. Harvey declared in an editorial for the *Washington Post* that "a reasonable level of divorce may be a symptom of a healthy and mobile society." Sure, long marriages can be rewarding for some couples. But for most of us, it's simply not "natural." Doesn't it make more sense, writes Harvey, to have different mates during various stages of life?

> Is it not possible that the ideal companion for our younger, child-rearing years will not be the ideal companion for our middle and later years? Is it not reasonable to suggest that the radical differences in the way we live in our fifties and sixties and beyond may be, under many circumstances, most appropriately lived with a different person from the one with whom we reared children?[4]

Manhattan psychotherapist Dr. David M. Fromm doubts whether 30-plus years with one spouse is "natural." He calls life-long marriage an "old-fashioned idea." Why? "People really need to feel fulfilled.... I think ultimately it's individuals [rather than families] that are the foundation of society."[5]

Articles like this make me wonder why Jo and I are still committed to our marriage after 30 years. Why do I stay with her when she's in a snippy mood at a certain time of the month? Why do I stay with her when she's so busy shuttling kids to school and activities, managing the household, and trying to write her own books that I can't convince her to drop everything for a romantic interlude? I can't say I'm deliriously happy at those moments.

A far more amazing question is why Jo remains committed to me. What causes her to stay with me when I'm so obsessed with work that my mind isn't home even when my body is? What causes her to stay with me when I snuggle next to her late at night and snore so loudly she can't sleep? What causes her to stay with me when I explode in anger because, being no Mr. Fixit, I can't repair a simple plumbing problem?

Those who know us might explain why we stay together by pointing to Scripture. They could refer to familiar Bible passages such as Genesis 2:24, which says a man shall leave his father and mother and cleave to his wife, or Malachi 2:16, where God says He hates divorce, or Ephesians 5, where wives are exhorted to submit to their husbands, and husbands are ordered to love their wives.

Certainly those are important verses to us, but none of these passages mentions happiness. Is it assumed? Or, once we're married, do we just grin and bear it? Obviously some of our Christian friends aren't willing to stick it out. They may acknowledge the same verses as we do, but if they're miserable at home, they seem intent on finding an escape clause for their marriage. Are Jo and I any different? Or are we also vulnerable to the forces that tear other couples apart?

Looking for Help

During the course of my career as a writer, editor, and publisher, I have known many wonderful teachers on the subject of marriage. Back in 1980, Jo and I hosted a conference for a dozen couples in Portland, Oregon. The speaker, Gary Smalley, was conducting just his second marriage seminar. Gary's messages have greatly encouraged Jo and me over the years, and millions have benefited from his "Keys to Loving Relationships" videos and conferences. We have also sat under the teaching of Dennis Rainey and others from FamilyLife seminars. We have interacted with outstanding authors like James Dobson, Scott Stanley, John Trent, Kevin Leman, Archibald Hart, Mike Mason, and many more. Each of them has enriched our marriage. They've provided the tools we need for effective communication, problem solving, and intimacy, plus encouragement to stay the course. Certainly there are more than enough seminars, books, research findings, diagnostic tools, tape series, and radio programs addressing the needs of marriage to aid any couple that wants help.

Yet all of that wonderful information won't keep a couple

together if they believe that unhappiness is a good enough reason to separate. We've never heard more great tips about how to have better sex, communications, financial planning, anger management, or goal setting. Still marriages continue to fail.

While I was writing this book, a nationally known ministry leader—someone Jo and I know personally—was exposed for having an affair. We were shocked, and Jo grieved for a week. On long walks, we talked about this couple. What had gone wrong? How could this man have violated his wedding vows? Were there warning signs that could have alerted someone and perhaps prevented this tragedy? Jo particularly worried about the man's wife, telling me how devalued she must certainly feel.

There is no doubt that this leader had enough information to protect and build his own marriage. He'd met most of the same marriage communicators I've known. He'd read their books and heard their teaching. But that knowledge didn't prevent his moral failure. Was it because he was unhappy or unfulfilled? It probably goes back to Jim's question: Does the promise to remain faithful "till death do us part" go out the window if we're miserable?

Lately, there has been a welcome increase in talk about commitment to lifelong marriage. A coalition of 50 organizations has produced the Covenant Marriage Movement. FamilyLife Ministries has conducted "I Still Do!" conferences in large arenas. Focus on the Family has as one of its six pillars a commitment to the permanence of marriage. But is a promise enough to keep a marriage going? What do we say to someone like Jim who believes he has made a terrible mistake? Or to the wife of the ministry leader who has fallen morally: Why should she stick it out?

That's why I've had to find an answer to Jim's question. Not just for him and Bonnie, not just for my friends, but for my own marriage as well. Toward that end, Jo and I have observed long-term marriages. We've smiled at the couple in their nineties, married more than 70 years, that still act like two teenagers on their first date. We've admired another couple that endured some rough times to raise five kids and in retirement now have a vibrant outreach to their community. We've noted the faithful wife whose husband suffered permanent brain damage 23 years ago, and how she has cared for him and honored him. Or the couple whose daughter suffers from life-threatening medical problems, who faithfully work together day after day even though he's lost his job. Each time we view such long-term committed marriages, our hearts are warmed and we feel intuitively that this is how it should be. These couples have endured far tougher problems than those of Jim and Bonnie. Why did they succeed when others in similar or easier circumstances failed?

I've also studied the Bible, read books, and attended more than 35 seminars to try and gain a sense of God's perspective on marriage. My questions were very simple. Why did God create marriage? And was it for our happiness? I knew that if ever a couple should have experienced happiness, it was the original couple in Eden. Assuming they did so, perhaps I could determine why, and that might provide insight into how happiness and marriage go together.

I am a writer and storyteller, not a theologian. So after immersing myself in the writings, teachings, and commentaries of biblical scholars and church fathers, I have attempted to "translate" all of that information into a form that communicates to me—that is, story. What follows in chapter two is the first of nine biblical vignettes or pictures that I want us to observe together. In between each drama we will search to understand the meaning of marriage.

2

An Original Creation

The verse in Genesis is beautiful but rather matter-of-fact, conveying little in the way of emotion.

> God created man in his own image,
> in the image of God he created him;
> male and female he created them.[1]

One day while reading again these familiar lines, I recalled the phrase "Even angels long to look into these things." That verse in 1 Peter, like several other verses in Scripture, implies that the angels observe from heaven the drama playing out on earth. I wondered what the angels saw at the time of Creation. What was their perspective on the first couple?[2]

Perhaps because of my experience at sporting events, for the first vignette I imagined the angels in a stadium, watching the Creation drama unfold...

The stadium was packed, and an ecstatic murmur ran up and down the stands. No one was seated, for the crowd knew that the Creator, the focus of their attention, was about to embark on His greatest work.

For some time now, the crowd had watched in awe. First, there was the formation of a dark ball of rock. Then a sudden flash of light illuminated the sphere. Next came the formation of water, followed by land, then plants, animals in the sea, birds of the air, and finally animals on the land. Each new addition was met with a rousing chorus of cheers and praise to the Almighty One, who needed only to speak and this remarkable world came into being.

Abdiel squeezed through the crowd and stood next to his friend Zephon. "Have I missed anything?" he eagerly asked.

"No. He's just started."

A hush fell over the audience as the All-Powerful One gathered a pile of rich, dark-red dirt and shaped it into an oval mound. He added a scoop of water and began to mix it with the dirt until it was a pliable hill of clay. Then, meticulously, He began to mold the clay. The lower half He split into two parts; the upper portion started as one small mound, then expanded and divided into three parts— one large torso and two long, thin appendages. "Can you tell what He's making?" whispered Abdiel.

"No. Let's be quiet and watch," Zephon answered.

With the basic shape established, the Creator moved purposefully, beginning at the head. Abdiel and Zephon stared as they saw a face emerge. Lovingly, the Creator shaped a nose, eyes, ears, and mouth. No detail was too trivial; He lingered over each part until He was completely satisfied.

After the head was completed, the Sculptor moved to the torso. The arms were fashioned, bent at the elbows. He lingered over the fingers, shaping them more finely than the paws on any other creature. He carefully made the thumb and forefinger so they touched at their tips. The Creator smiled at this small detail. The huge crowd was hushed as their Master continued His work. He shaped the feet, taking time to form each individual toe, pausing after each to savor His handiwork.

At last the sculpture was completed. The angels gasped and applauded the beauty of this model. Spontaneous shouts and cheers erupted until the Creator held up His hand, and the crowd collectively held its breath. The Artist bent over His sculpture, touched the mouth with His, and breathed into the form. Then He stepped back so His audience could observe as the chest began moving slowly, rhythmically up and down.

"This is no ordinary creature," whispered Abdiel. "He's never breathed His breath into another."

The creation then opened its eyes, and the Artist held out His hand and pulled the creature to his feet.

"Do you see what He's doing?" said Zephon, who restrained himself from shouting for joy as realization set in.

"It's amazing! But what is it?" answered Abdiel. "The other animals are beautiful, yet this one is different."

"I don't think this is an animal. Let's watch! We will understand soon enough."

The angels couldn't help but stare, for never had they seen such a wonder. The other creatures were an incredible array of form and beauty, but this one was unique. The creature stumbled for a moment, but quickly, like a newborn colt, gained the use of his legs. The Creator smiled and said, "You are Adam. Come! Let Me show you what I have prepared for you."

Then the Creator led His creature to a garden, the lushest, most beautiful place in this young world. Each tree was full and green, many bearing colorful flowers, each with its fruit. There were apples and pears and apricots and oranges and bananas and man-goes and figs and dates—on and on. The variety was astounding. It was a feast for eyes, nose, and tongue.

Sweeping His arm to take in all the beauty, the Creator said to Adam, "This is yours to live in. Take good care of it!" Then like a proud gardener, He led the man slowly through the orchard, point-ing out each kind of tree. "Take one!" He said several times. "Taste it! Do you like it?" He described the traits of each fruit and men-tioned how to care for each tree. Some would require pruning to maximize the bearing of fruit. Others required cultivating the soil beneath the branches, for the grass would eventually invade that space. The man took in each piece of information, eager to know everything possible about each tree and its fruit.

Then the two reached the center of the garden, where a majes-tic river flowed. Next to the river were two unique and wondrous trees. They stopped to gaze. "The one tree is the tree of life," the Creator announced. "The other is the tree of the knowledge of good and evil." Again the Creator swept His arm to show the man His garden. "You are free to eat from any tree in the garden!" He said. Then He pointed to the second of the two trees by the river. "But you must not eat from the tree of the knowledge of good and evil, for when you eat of it you will surely die."

A momentary feeling of dread washed over Abdiel. It was an emotion he'd felt only once before, during the rebellion, but it didn't make sense now in the context of such joy. He couldn't imag-ine the man wanting to disobey his Creator, who was happier than Abdiel had ever seen Him before. "Our Master delights in this crea-ture, more than in all the others," he observed to his friend.

"Yes," agreed Zephon. "Do you see yet what makes this creation unique?"

"If I didn't know better, I'd almost think this Adam is like our Lord, at least in some respects."

"Yes, you are beginning to see," said Zephon.

Abdiel laughed, for his friend always recognized and understood what God was doing sooner than he did. That made sense, for Zephon's name meant "search" or "discover," while Abdiel was simply "God's servant." This hierarchy never frustrated him; Zephon was created able to recognize such things sooner, yet he never spoiled it by explaining what he saw unless his friend asked. Though it took longer, Abdiel wanted to make as many discoveries as possible for himself. Zephon respected that.

There was a stirring in the stands, and Abdiel turned his attention back to the drama unfolding in the garden on planet Earth. "It is not good for the man to be alone," announced the Creator. "I will make a helper suitable for him." Abdiel wondered if "the man" knew for whom this was spoken, since the Creator didn't seem to be speaking this to the man, and the man was apparently unaware of the heavenly host observing every facet of this drama.

Abdiel laughed with joy, for the Creator wasn't finished. Yet how could He possibly fashion anything more beautiful than what they'd already witnessed? Never had such wonders been seen by the angels. Never had their Master demonstrated such excitement. But Abdiel didn't understand the emotion of the Creator. It was as though the Creator had a surprise He wanted to reveal to Adam. But what was it? The Master sure wasn't in a hurry to reveal it; rather it was almost like a game. Again the host of heaven was hushed as they watched.

The Creator told the man to wait while He went away for a moment. Shortly He returned, leading two animals. They were sleek and gold in color, one with a full mane framing its oval face, the other slimmer, more finely boned. Like a proud artist showing off various pieces in his gallery, He presented the animals. "What do you think?" He said to the man.

"They are beautiful!" exclaimed Adam.

"What would you call them?" asked God.

The man looked into the face of the two animals, then walked slowly around them, studying their every detail. "They are different, yet of the same kind," he observed.

"That's right! The bigger one is male, the other female."

"I would say they are lions!" Adam finally answered.

"Yes, perfect!" said God. The male lion opened wide its mouth in a yawn, then the pair strolled away.

"Would you like to see something else?" said the Creator.

"Yes, by all means!"

God slipped away again and brought another animal for the man, one much smaller than the lion, with colorful feathers instead of fur. He held up the creature, which flapped its wings for a moment and then perched patiently on the Creator's arm. "What do you think?" He asked Adam.

"I've observed others similar to this. I've seen them flying. This is a bird!"

"That's right. There are many birds. But what kind is this?"

Adam again studied the creature. "It has a large beak. Can it speak?"

"Yes, it can, but not like you. It can only copy your speech."

"Then I'll call it a parrot."

The bird cawed, "Call it a parrot," and both the Creator and the man laughed. With a flick of the Creator's arm, the parrot took flight and alighted on a nearby tree.

"Isn't this fun!" said the Creator. "Shall we do some more?" He was already heading away from Adam to find another creature.

The heavenly host was amazed. They had never seen the Creator interact with any angels or creatures in this way. With the heavenly host, He was Lord over all but intimate with none. God was positively giddy. God and man were sharing an intimacy that could almost make Abdiel jealous, for who wouldn't want to know the Creator in this manner! Abdiel commented to his friend, "This Adam is not a servant like us."

"No," agreed Zephon. "He is more fragile. He certainly has a different purpose from us. He has something unique that we don't. Do you see it?"

"No, but don't tell me. I will discover it myself!"

Like a dance, the Creator and Adam related. Pairs of elephants, kangaroos, ostrich, zebras, horses, sheep, giraffes—each were brought to the man, who studied them and gave them names. God seemed to enjoy the process of sharing His creation, and neither tired of the process as new animals appeared for Adam to examine and name.

At last God stopped and asked, "So which one would you like? Which one would make a suitable helper for my Adam?"

The man shook his head and nearly laughed at the absurdity of the question.

"No," God agreed, "none is right for you." This, too, was like a game where God already knew the answer but wanted the man to recognize the same truth for himself. Abdiel was enraptured by the scene.

"Lie down," God said to Adam. The man obeyed, lying among the trees on a rich bed of grass. Instantly, the man fell into a deep sleep, and the Creator went to work. He opened up the man's side and quickly snapped off one of his ribs. Then with a swipe of His hand, He closed the wound.

Abdiel and all the angels leaned forward to see what their Lord was doing, but this time the Creator blocked their view as He worked on the rib. He took His time but finally stepped aside to reveal His work. Abdiel shouted with the others, for this was, if possible, a more glorious sight, a creature even more beautiful, more graceful, more delicate than the man. The Creator smiled and led the creature to where Adam lay sleeping. He gently shook the man's shoulder and Adam awoke. "Look!" urged the Creator.

Abdiel had never seen such an expression of astonishment. It was as though all the other creatures Adam had seen paled in light of this new creation. As he gazed on this person, the Creator proudly standing aside, Adam felt his side, then exclaimed, "This is bone of my bones and flesh of my flesh!" The created one understood the process now. The Creator fashioned; Adam observed and named.

"She shall be called woman, for she was taken out of man."

Adam stared at her and grinned. The woman bowed her head and blushed with pleasure.

God seemed pleased. Yes, this was good. This was as good as it gets!

As Abdiel gazed at the man and woman, a realization began to dawn on him. "Zephon, I think I see something incredible. It's amazing!"

The higher-ranking angel smiled and said, "I thought I saw it in the man. But that was only part of it."

"Yes, there is something about the two of them *together*. You see part of the image in the man. Physically strong. Bold. Reasoning."

"Each trait a reflection of our Master."

"But the man doesn't have them all. Look at the woman. The beauty. Tenderness. Softness."

"And did you notice they have personality? I've seen it in the man, but it's different in the woman."

"And the emotions—it's as though He wants them to *feel* what He is feeling."

"Yes, they're somehow supposed to experience His creation as He sees it. I'm sure we can't begin to understand it all, yet. The unique differences between the man and the woman will become clearer over time."

"Oh, look how He is bringing them together!" The two angels became silent as their Master took the hand of the man and the hand of the woman and joined them. It was obviously a ceremony. "Man and wife" He pronounced them. "The two shall become one flesh."

Then Abdiel understood. "This is truly His greatest work."

"His masterpiece!" said Zephon. "Together, they reflect the Creator better than either could separately."

"Amazing." Abdiel watched as God stepped back, glowing in pride, and the man and woman gazed at each other, touching only their fingertips. "Yes, God has created two like Himself..."

"Not exactly like Him," corrected Zephon.

"No, not the same. Yet, you see glimpses of Him in the two of them together."

Zephon understood. "Yes, He is three yet one. They are two yet one."

"Two, maybe. But with the Creator that makes three!"

By now, all of the angelic audience saw what Abdiel and Zephon had recognized. In this man and woman, joined together, God had provided a reflection of Himself for all His creation. Two incredible creatures, brilliant and beautiful, each unique, but together revealing deeper aspects of the intricate beauty of their Creator.

Truly, this was a work of art. This was God's masterpiece.

3

Analyzing the
Masterpiece

When Michelangelo stood below the ceiling of the Sistine Chapel
and gazed at his completed work; when Beethoven finished his
ninth symphony; when John Bunyan penned the last words of *The
Pilgrim's Progress*—they caught a microscopic hint of the joy the
Creator felt on the first day of human history. Just as the artist, composer, and author desire an audience with whom to share their creation, for this defining moment of human history God required an
uproariously appreciative crowd. Who else could yell "Bravo!"
besides His angels?

But something strikes me about this moment. I seem far more
aware of God's happiness than that of the two people. The only outburst of human emotion is Adam's exclamation of awe when he is
introduced to his helper. After that, we're not told whether Adam
and Eve were happy. However, God seems quite pleased. For all His
other creations, God said they were good. But after creating man
and woman and placing them in the midst of the garden, He

declared they were "very good." Until the Incarnation, no greater praise was uttered. God certainly relished His handiwork.

Why did He do it? Why did God create us?

Why does any true artist create? In today's market-driven society there is much "art" created solely for commercial profit. I'm talking about something much greater, about writers and composers and painters who try to connect with our soul. With great art, I feel I'm somehow linked to the creator. Listening to the adagio movement of Bach's concerto for two violins, I feel mystically joined to a composer who lived 300 years ago. Reading *My Name is Asher Lev* by Chaim Potok, I identify with the author's struggle to be faithful to his art and his Jewish faith. For me, art is an act of self-expression, revealing the heart of the artist, disclosing the creator's deepest thoughts and desires, thereby allowing me to enter into his world.

If that is correct, why did God create the first couple? The man and woman weren't playthings or even pets that might sit at His feet in adoration like a pair of golden retrievers. These were independent entities who could love Him or reject Him. God, who needed nothing, apparently desired something that could be freely given and freely shared.

What Did God Want?

In a very small way, I can try to understand the Artist's intent by imagining the wealthiest man in the world living on an estate of immense size, with thousands of servants, land the size of a country, and every imaginable need met. Suppose, however, that he desires to share his abundant life with others who freely choose to accept and enjoy it. He wants to give himself in love to some friends. Sure, he has his paid servants, but how can he find genuine companionship with them? He desires to pour out his love on people with whom he can experience the deepest intimacy, who will enjoy his bounty, who will respond in gratitude for who he is and not simply for his gifts.

Within the Trinity, there was already perfect relationship, and the Godhead had no needs whatsoever. But God definitely wanted something. He desired intimacy with people who could choose whether or not to love Him back.

One might wonder why God didn't choose to focus His attention on beings more powerful than humans. God is surrounded by angels, the least of whom is mightier than the strongest man. Did He make us frail because God wanted to provide everything for His special creatures? Is it because He wanted to demonstrate His love to someone who could give Him nothing except love in return?

Or consider another challenge. God is so great, so awesome, so powerful. How could such a delicate creature as a human being relate to Him? Perhaps that is why God made man and woman and united them as husband and wife. Only together, in their relationship with each other, would they begin to understand the God who wanted to love them. And perhaps, within their intimacy, in their oneness, man and woman would begin to understand how they could relate to the awesome Creator.

All that helps me understand why God made us and how we might relate to Him. But it doesn't address Jim's question. He claimed God wanted him to be happy, and he wasn't happy married to Bonnie.

So how did the first couple feel about being created? Were they happy in this paradise? "Of course they were happy!" most of us answer. Who wouldn't be? If marriage is primarily about happiness, then Adam and Eve had to be the happiest couple in history.

It is logical to assume that the Creator desired their happiness. Consider that He gave them all the things we as humans want.

He gave them a great purpose: "Be fruitful and increase in number; fill the earth and subdue it."[1]

28   your
m a r r i a g e
masterpiece

He provided for their needs: "I give you every seed-bearing plant on the face of the whole earth and every tree that has fruit with seed in it. They will be yours for food."[2]

He gave them pleasure: "The man and his wife were both naked, and they felt no shame."[3]

He gave them a chance to know Him: "God created man in his own image...; male and female he created them"[4]; and "the man and his wife heard the sound of the Lord God as he was walking in the garden in the cool of the day."[5]

I can't help imagining what life was like for them. I've tried to put myself in their skin and imagine life together with my wife without any hint of stress, in a perfect world where we are free to explore, all our needs are met, and there is daily interaction with the Creator Himself. The angels might observe this, but they can't feel what the first couple felt.

It was early evening in Eden. A tired first couple lounged against two large walnut trees. The woman had an orange and dug into the peel with her fingers, releasing a fragrant mist that she joyfully inhaled and savored. Adam broke the skin of a pomegranate and popped a handful of juicy seeds into his mouth. The flavor of the fruit exploded on his tongue and the roof of his mouth, and Adam closed his eyes to enjoy the sensation.

As Adam started to recall the events of the day, his reverie was interrupted by something soft hitting his foot. Adam opened his eyes and looked at his wife, who was popping another slice of orange into her mouth. He dug out another clump of pomegranate seeds to eat and closed his eyes again. This time he felt something hit his chest. He looked down and saw a piece of orange rind lying on his stomach.

Eve continued to eat her orange as though nothing had happened, looking into the distance. Adam felt for a clean seed, formed his mouth into a small opening and fired the seed with his tongue, hitting his wife on her thigh. She giggled but continued to look away. Then with a flick of her wrist, another orange peel flew toward her husband. He ducked and fired another seed. Eve started laughing, stood and flung the remainder of her peels at her husband, who promptly rose and started to chase her.

Eve dashed ahead of Adam until she took a sharp turn around an apple tree and suddenly stopped. Adam wrapped his arms around his wife to break his own run and looked up to see what had halted the chase—the person of the Creator, who was grinning at the scene. The three were still giggling as they all sat down and lounged on a lush patch of grass.

When the laughter had died away, they sat in silence, enjoying the whisper of a breeze through the trees. A short distance away, they could hear the river gently flowing. The three were supremely happy and content.

Finally the Lord spoke. "So you had a good day?"

"Oh, yes!" Eve responded. "It was our best day yet!"

The Creator chuckled. "You say that every day."

"It's true. There is so much to see, to do, to learn."

Gently, the Creator said, "Tell me all about it."

Adam and Eve started talking at the same time, then stopped. All three laughed, and Adam said, "You go first!"

Eve rose up on her knees in order to better express herself with her hands. "Well, I woke up and Adam had already risen. I could see him hurrying back, carrying something in his hands. 'Look what I discovered!' he said, and he laid these most beautiful red pieces of fruit down in front of me."

Adam picked up his cue. "They're only so round," Adam said, holding his thumb and forefinger about an inch apart, "and they hung from these stems about this long." Again he held up his thumb and forefinger about two inches apart.

30   your
m a r r i a g e
masterpiece

"I had to gaze at them before I tasted one," said Eve. "They are so perfectly formed. Adam took one by the stem and placed it in my mouth, then pulled the stem back. I rolled the little piece of fruit in my mouth for a moment, then bit into it."

Adam could hardly contain himself. "What a marvelous flavor! We took our time slowly chewing the pulp off the seed. Eve named it."

"Cherries! They are so perfect, so tasty. Can You tell us how You thought of them?"

The Lord laughed and leaned back. "I created them for your enjoyment, just as I created all the fruits in the garden. I thought of many flavors and shapes and sizes. I'm glad you like them. Cherries! What a perfect name!"

"Thank You!"

"What else did you see and do? Please, don't leave anything out. I want to hear it all!"

Adam started. "We were just finishing our morning meal when Eve saw something move out of the corner of her eye. She whispered and pointed. Through the trees, about 100 long steps away, in a grassy opening stood two beautiful animals. We walked around behind them until we were just a few steps away."

Eve took over the narration. "The female turned and looked at us. I slowly walked toward her, not wanting to startle her. The animals were almost our height. The female had the most beautiful dark-brown eyes. She let me stroke her neck."

"We spent considerable time with them, for the sun was high when they separated. The male stood erect like this"—Adam stood and demonstrated—"and he had a rack of antlers, four points on each side."

"What did you call the animals?" the Creator asked.

"Deer," said Adam.

"They had white tails," Eve added. "I suggested we call them white-tailed deer."

"Then they cantered toward the river, so we followed them."

"They drank from the water, then trotted off, and we left them alone."

Adam got animated as he recalled the next part of the day. "I wanted to follow the river north—we had not explored that part of the garden. We walked a ways along the river until we came upon a stream flowing into the river, so we turned left and followed that stream to see where it would lead."

Eve continued: "About a thousand steps along that stream we came to a hill and what I call a waterfall—the stream was spilling over the hill and down some rocks. It was an absolutely beautiful spot!"

"We climbed up the rocks along the waterfall, though Eve wasn't sure she wanted to."

"It was a little steep. But I made it! And we had a wonderful view of part of the garden from the top of the hill."

"Then here's the best part. There was this incredible layer of thick moss by the stream, right before it spills over the side of the hill. It felt wonderful to lie down on, so we lay down together and—"

"Now Adam, are you going to tell everything?!"

"He said not to leave anything out. It was absolutely wonderful!"

Eve's face turned red, not from embarrassment but rather from the pleasure of that memory.

"You said we would become one," Adam said to the Creator. "I had no idea that it would mean such physical enjoyment. There is no other sensation like it!"

"Eve completes you, Adam," the Creator said. "She came out of your side—you, yourself, called her woman. This afternoon, you became one again."

Eve regained her composure and said, "When he was inside

32   your
m a r r i a g e
masterpiece

me, it was like he was part of me. He knew my thoughts and feelings, and I knew his."

"It seemed so natural," said Adam. "My whole body sang for
joy, and then I thought of You!"

"Yes, I, too, thought of You," said Eve.

"That was what I intended. You may enjoy each other as often
as you wish. And when you are joined, remember that we are one."

The man and wife instinctively reached out and held hands.
Adam then posed a question. "You have spoken often of Yourself in
the plural—we or us. I'd like to understand what that means. Could
you explain how You are one and several at the same time?"

"I was hoping you would ask Me!" The Creator sat up and
began to reveal more of Himself to His creation. The first couple
leaned forward and soaked in every word, not even noticing when
the sun had set and night settled over them.

Finally, when they could barely see each other, they heard Him
say, "We will talk more of these and many other things. I want you
to know Me better and better as time goes by. You may ask anything
you wish, and I will answer you. Now sleep well. Sleep deep, and
rest for the joys tomorrow will bring."

Searching for God's Intention

So were Adam and Eve happy? I've tried to imagine their joy, and
I'm sure my imagination doesn't begin to express what they really
experienced. I have to believe God expected them to be happy.

However, there are some elements that add nuance to the question. I notice that this first marriage was a three-way relationship.
This is implied in the visitation of God to the first man and woman
during the cool of the day. This appears to have been a normal pattern—each day after Adam and Eve finished their work and exploration, they debriefed with their Creator. What wonderful talks those

must have been. Imagine recounting your discovery of a new animal or plant to God and His sharing your excitement. Or the first couple asking questions of the Creator: Why did You create the giraffe with such a long neck? Why did You make plant leaves the color green? What is heaven like? Could we meet one of Your angels? Are there other worlds like this? The possibilities are endless.

God seems to have been totally involved in this marriage, beginning with the fact that God gave Eve to Adam and performed the marriage ceremony. The couple never dated. Adam never bent his knee and popped the question. Eve never had a romantic candlelight dinner before her honeymoon. It was simply assumed that the two were compatible and that they would live well together. If or when there were problems, it was expected they would work through them. Of course, it's also assumed that God would be there personally to guide them.

Second, it seems to me that marriage was supposed to be an exciting adventure that the husband and wife shared. We see this in God's initial instructions to the first man and woman. God blessed them and said to them, "Be fruitful and increase in number; fill the earth and subdue it. Rule over the fish of the sea and the birds of the air and over every living creature that moves on the ground."[6]

There is in this divine charge a sense of wonder and excitement. Imagine the entire unexplored world waiting to be discovered. This couple was placed in one minuscule area of the globe. The garden was their base of operation. I can imagine the excitement of eventually expanding their activities beyond that safe garden to discover the Nile River or the boot of Italy. Then they might move north into the Alps, or east toward the Himalayas, eventually climbing to the top of the world. They'd come to the oceans and devise a way to travel across those great bodies of water, eventually entering the Amazon or exploring the Grand Canyon. All this awaited both man and woman and their children. This was not a boring life spent tilling the ground, eking out a minimal existence. Life was adventure of the highest order, more than enough to challenge and excite any human.

I also see the possibilities for science as the couple sought to understand God's creation. Man and woman were commissioned to rule over God's living creatures. God Himself is the great King of the universe, ruling over the angelic beings and all of His creation. Man and woman were to share in this experience by ruling the earth. But how does one rule without understanding? Adam and Eve and their offspring would need to explore, study, and learn all about the creation. Science was there on the first day of human history; it included study of trees and plants, the great animals, the fish of the sea, and insects. It meant learning the laws of chemistry and physics. These weren't ignorant creatures who needed to evolve, but highly intelligent beings with the potential for discovering the laws of relativity and quantum mechanics. There was so much to learn if they were to truly understand and rule wisely.

There was further shared adventure in the responsibility of bearing and raising children. The first couple were expected to be fruitful and increase in number. In the process of parenting, Adam and Eve were to pass along this wonderful vision for the world. They were to prepare their progeny for adventure and knowledge and exploration. No initial instructions were given in how to parent—the first couple were expected to work together and learn how to do it, no doubt in regular consultation with their Creator.

All of this was a joint commission. We might call it a "relational adventure." The man wasn't just going off by himself to explore, leaving the wife home to tend to the kids. She and their children would join the great adventure and help rule this world. Adam would help train the children, preparing them for their responsibilities as adults. And God would always be there to counsel, to point them in the right direction, and to share their excitement over each discovery.

In His Image

Third, marriage was, in some mysterious way, supposed to be a reflection of God. The Genesis account says, "God created man in his own image, in the image of God he created him; male and female he created them."[7] This leads to so many questions. If man and woman reflect the image of the Creator, just what do we learn about God as we watch them relate as husband and wife? And what are the means by which we will see this image?

Perhaps we gain a clue with God's statement that a man must leave his father and mother and "be united to his wife, and they will become one flesh."[8] This is indeed a mystery, how two can become one, for obviously the husband and wife retain their individual characteristics. Steve Tracy, a professor of theology and ethics at Phoenix Seminary, has specialized in sexual issues, beginning with his ministry to singles as an associate pastor before he became a professor. In an interview with *Christianity Today*, he observed:

> In many cases, singles have been redefining what sex is and what's appropriate. What I'm seeing played out is a depersonalization of human beings through sexual behaviors and practices. The divine intent is total intimacy. It's to know as opposed to lie with. "To lie with" is an Old Testament phrase for inappropriate sexual behavior. However, in the Genesis context it's yada—"to know"—a beautiful term for complete sharing, not just of bodies but of souls.[9]

In the biblical act of knowing one another, a couple become literally one flesh at the moment of intercourse. And in the fruit of their union a new creation emerges. In this we get a taste of how we, as God's children, reflect His image, for children are a reflection of the image of both parents. Plus, we see in a healthy marriage how a husband and wife, while retaining their distinctiveness, begin to understand each other and even think like the other thinks, so that eventually the union becomes stronger than either individual. It's not uncommon even to recognize a growing physical resemblance among spouses who have been married many years. In a small way, this oneness in marriage reflects the unity within the Trinity.

One writer who seems to have captured this mystery is Mike Mason. In his classic book *The Mystery of Marriage*, he defines marriage as "the contemplation of the love of God in and through the form of another human being."[10] Later, he writes:

> To "fall in love" actually means (whether or not a person cares to admit this) to have a revelation from God. It is to receive from Him a new vision as to the true nature of things, and new insight into the power and potential of life.... That is what is so distressing about divorce: it separates the divorcé not only from his mate, but in many ways from his own religion.[11]

All this suggests that happiness and self-fulfillment were natural by-products of marriage as God intended it, but not the primary purpose for marriage. The first marriage was at least as much about relating to God as it was about relating to each other.

However, I can't help but note that only this marriage existed in a perfect environment, and the couple certainly didn't live happily ever after. Adam and Eve apparently were happy, or at least content, until Satan suggested that they should have something more—something he implied was very good, that they deserved, that they needed. Satan's message was "God is holding out on you. You don't have it all."

Discontent has existed in marriages ever since.

4

Adam's Greatest Moment

The serpent must have exploited some need. Had Eve become bored? Had the man become restless, perhaps wanting to expand beyond the restrictions of the garden? Did the two think something was lacking? Perhaps, on several occasions, they separately looked at the tree of the knowledge of good and evil, wondering, What if...?

I imagine Adam and Eve exploring one day in the garden. As Adam examined the delicate flower of a fruit tree, Eve wandered away. Something had caught her eye, and she headed toward the two trees in the center of the garden. Suddenly she stopped; on the bank of the river stood a magnificent animal. It's futile to speculate about what the serpent looked like, but obviously he could speak, and he probably charmed Eve in some way. Was Eve suspicious of this talking beast? Did he relax her defenses by flattery?

The Genesis account gets right to the heart of the conflict. The serpent said to the first woman, "Did God really say, 'You must not eat from any tree in the garden'?" By this point, Adam has joined his

*wife—the Scriptures are clear on this detail—and he heard the criti-
cal dialogue between them.*[1]

We all know what happened next. Both Adam and Eve took the
bait. Both tasted the fruit. But I have often wondered what could have
happened. Surely, the first man and woman weren't destined to fall.
Each had freedom to choose, regardless of what the other did. Is there
any insight to be gained about marriage by looking at this situation
from a hypothetical perspective? That is the purpose of our second
vignette.

Adam and Eve gazed at the beautiful creature as he spoke: "Did
God really say, 'You must not eat from any tree in the garden'?"

Eve caught the twist in the serpent's question and answered,
"We may eat fruit from the trees in the garden, but God did say, 'You
must not eat fruit from the tree that is in the middle of the garden,
and you must not touch it, or you will die.'"

Adam interrupted to correct his wife: "Eve, dear, God didn't say
we couldn't touch the fruit from the tree of the knowledge of good
and evil. He only said that if we ate of it, we would surely die."

"You will not die," the serpent lied to the woman, ignoring
Adam's intrusion. "For God knows that when you eat of it your eyes
will be opened, and you will be like God, knowing good and evil."

The woman didn't respond but simply stared at the tree. Adam,
on her behalf, confronted the serpent. "You do not speak rightly.
God said we would surely die. Look around us! God has given us
everything in this garden, and we are free to eat any fruit except for
the fruit of this single tree. How can you possibly suggest that we
disobey the One who made us and gave us all that we have?"

But Eve wasn't listening to her husband, and the serpent
ignored the protestations when he saw that Eve couldn't take her
eyes off the fruit. She studied it as she had studied the fruit of other

trees, and she could see that this was pleasant to look at, good to eat, and in fact, very desirable. Her thirst for knowledge, which had served her so well throughout the garden, now drew her to the forbidden fruit.

Adam could see what was happening and tried to warn her: "Don't listen to the serpent, Eve! Let's leave here. Don't even think about eating from that tree."

It was too late. Eve reached out and plucked the fruit. The serpent grinned and stepped away. Adam was horrified, feeling fear for the first time. "No! This is not right." For a moment, Adam wondered if he should forcibly remove the fruit from her hand, but he was so shocked that he couldn't move. He pleaded with his wife: "Please, just drop it!"

There was a ritual the first couple had shared throughout the garden as they acquainted themselves with a new kind of fruit. First one would pluck a sample, take a bite and slowly chew it, analyzing the flavor. Then he or she would hand it to the partner, who would do the same. Together they would compare their observations. Was it sweet or tart, soft or chewy, smooth or textured? Did it have a covering that needed to be peeled, or could they bite right into it? How did it sit in the stomach? What were the effects on their bodies? They had categorized many fruits so far. In this manner, Eve took a bite of the fruit and carefully savored the taste as she chewed. Then she handed it to Adam to taste.

But Adam refused her offer. "No, we can't do this! God explicitly told us not to eat from this tree."

The serpent retreated a discreet distance to watch. Eve slyly looked up at her husband. "You really should eat," she said with a mischievous smile that had always captured his playful side. She took another bite. "It has a unique sweetness. You'll love it. Come on, honey. Just try one bite!"

Adam held up his hands and backed away. Eve stepped toward

40   your
m a r r i a g e
masterpiece

him, holding out the partially eaten fruit. Then she stopped, considering some new sensation. "I can see more clearly now! Yes, it's like my eyes are opened."

"What do you mean?" Adam asked, puzzled. "Our eyes are perfectly fine."

"No, this fruit definitely does something to the eyes. I can see things more clearly."

For the first time in his life, Adam was confused. What did his wife see? "What things? You had better explain."

"Well, for one thing, we're naked. We should cover ourselves."

"Of course we're naked! That's how we were created—we don't need any covering."

"Oh, silly, of course we do." Eve sprang into action. She casually tossed the fruit to her husband and headed toward the fig tree.

Adam jumped sideways and let the partially eaten fruit fall to the ground. Then he ran after Eve. "Stop! What are you talking about?"

Eve pulled down some leaves and wove them together by their stems. She placed the apron around her waist and turned to pose for her husband. "What do you think?"

"What do I think? This is crazy. Why are you covering yourself with leaves? You don't need any covering!"

Eve ignored Adam's protests and pulled down another branch to weave together a covering for her breasts. "Why are you worrying?" she laughed. "The serpent was right." She turned and confronted Adam. "I'm not going to die. Look at me! I'm just as alive as before. More alive, in fact! For the first time, I see things clearly. I'd say God has been holding back from us."

"What do you mean?" Adam said.

"Just what the serpent said. I'm like God now! I recognize the difference between good and evil. For example, I know you really should cover that body of yours."

Adam had never felt such perplexity. He had no idea how to answer his wife. At times he'd had questions, and always in those situations he'd taken them to God. It was late in the day, and God would be coming soon to meet with them. Adam said nothing but turned his head to listen for the familiar sound he so loved and anticipated each evening. There it was, a rustling in the leaves, coming closer. He turned back to Eve. She was gone. "Eve, where are you?" he shouted. Then he heard her scampering away from him among the trees.

Even greater fear washed over Adam. One part of him wanted to go after Eve. But the stronger pull was toward God. Where else could he go to settle this confusion? He ran toward the sound of his Creator and burst into a clearing to meet Him face-to-face. The Lord warmly greeted him. "Adam! It is so good to see you. But, where is Eve?"

"She is hiding," Adam answered, breathing hard.

"Why is she hiding?"

Adam fell on his knees and felt tears begin to flow for the first time. "Lord, she has done a terrible thing. She has eaten of the tree that You commanded us not to eat from. I tried to stop her, but she did it anyway. I do not know what to do."

The Lord called out to the woman, "Eve, where are you?" Adam shuddered at the voice; there was a hint of harshness he'd never heard before.

There was a moment of silence, then Adam heard Eve say, "I heard You coming, and I was afraid because I was naked; so I hid."

Adam had never heard fear in the voice of his wife, and again he felt the sting of tears as God spoke: "Who told you that you were naked? Have you eaten from the tree that I commanded you not to eat from?" The leaves of the trees in the garden seemed to shudder at the sound of God's anger.

"The serpent deceived me, and I ate," she answered.

"Please, Lord," Adam said. "Will she really die?"

The Lord looked on the man He had created and said, "She must!"

"But how can I live without her?" The tears flowed even harder. "She is such a wonderful helper."

"I will make you another helper," God said.

"But, Lord…" Adam hesitated, understanding for the first time a new emotion. "I want *my wife*, not another. I *love* her. Isn't there anything You can do?"

"Surely I made it clear! When you eat of the tree of the knowledge of good and evil, you will die. And so she must. Unless…"

Adam looked up hopefully. "Unless what?"

"One can die in her place. One who hasn't disobeyed my command."

A feeling of dread fell over Adam, but it couldn't overwhelm his love for Eve. "Lord, there is no other but me." Then, not thinking of the consequences, he blurted out the words "Take me instead of her."

Adam felt a hand on his shoulder and looked up into the face of his Lord and friend. There were tears in His eyes as well. "I know you love her. It is not necessary for you to die. There is another who will die in her place."

5

Every Marriage Needs a Hero

What went wrong in the garden? And what, if anything, does that have to do with my marital happiness?

Apparently the first couple didn't think paradise was enough. They wanted the one thing God had withheld from them, the knowledge of good and evil. The sad fact is that when they got what they wanted, it did not make them happy.

The wife, in the process of childbearing, supposedly one of her greatest moments of joy, received increased pain.

The husband, rather than living out the great adventure, had to work hard in order to gain the food his family needed for subsistence. Pain and sweat were introduced into his daily life. What once came effortlessly was now a source of frustration. When he tried to raise fruits and vegetables, sometimes he got thorns and thistles.

The wife, instead of obtaining her desire for a full-fledged partnership with her husband, gained a ruler. Instead of ruling the world with her husband, she was claimed as his consolation prize.

44   your
m a r r i a g e
masterpiece

We can conclude that whatever happiness Adam and Eve desired was not attained by disobeying God and eating the forbidden fruit.

However, it didn't have to happen. The point of my speculation in the previous chapter is that even if one succumbed to temptation, the spouse didn't have to fall. Adam could have tried to stop Eve. Of course, she freely chose to eat from the forbidden tree. The Scriptures make it clear that she was deceived by the serpent.[1] But Adam wasn't deceived. Augustine wrote in his classic *The City of God*:

> Eve accepted the serpent's word as true, whereas Adam refused
> to be separated from his partner even in a union of sin—not,
> of course, that he was, on that account, any less guilty, since
> he sinned knowingly and deliberately. That is why the Apostle
> does not say: "He did not sin," but "he was not deceived."[2]

So if Adam understood the situation, he had some options. He could passively let his wife succumb to the temptation. He could be an active participant with her in the tasting of the fruit. Or he could intervene and resist the tempter. Failing that, he could plead with his wife. If she insisted on eating the fruit, he could refuse her invitation to eat, and appeal on her behalf to the Creator. Instead, Adam stood by and watched and listened to the tempter, then passively let his wife experiment by taking the first taste of the fruit.

Adam was positioned to be the hero of this story by trying to prevent the tragedy or, failing that, pleading to God on behalf of his wife. What would God have thought of Adam's offer? Wouldn't He have been pleased? How would Eve have felt about her husband's intercession? Might it have broken her heart? Maybe she would have seen the horror of her misdeed and repented, begging God for mercy. Sure, God would have had to act on His word—there was a consequence for disobedience that couldn't be ignored. However, we also know that God planned before the creation of the world to provide a redeemer by having His Son take the place of all offenders and pay the penalty for their disobedience.[3]

Of course, Adam wasn't a hero. Just the opposite: He was a coward! Adam let his wife face the deception of the serpent while he only watched and listened. When she picked the fruit, he made no effort to stop her. I wonder if secretly he wanted to taste of the fruit just as much as she did but was afraid to do so. Perhaps he was concerned about those words "for when you eat of it you will surely die." Was he letting Eve do the dirty work—seeing how she reacted to tasting the forbidden fruit? When it seemed there were no poisonous effects, only then did he also take and eat of the fruit.

Meeting Each Other's Needs

What did the first man and first woman need from each other? Adam needed a wife who would simply trust God and obey Him, even if she didn't understand the reason for His prohibition. Eve could have questioned the serpent's words. She could have sought to understand better the Lord's instructions. Instead, she succumbed to the serpent's spell. She didn't try to understand God's instructions (in fact, she added the words "you must not touch it"). She was certainly no help to Adam in this moment of temptation— she might have discerned what was happening but didn't try. Instead she believed someone she didn't know, rather than turning to Adam or God, whom she did know.

What did Eve need? She needed a hero. Adam should have recognized the danger and stepped in to protect his wife. He probably knew God's command better than Eve did. It was to Adam that God gave the command "you must not eat from the tree of the knowledge

46   your
m a r r i a g e
masterpiece

of good and evil."[4] There is no indication that God repeated that instruction to Eve. So it was Adam's responsibility to protect Eve by making sure she understood God's law.

Adam could have exposed the serpent's deception. Instead he proved himself a coward. At the first sign of danger to a young world, he who was supposed to rule instead surrendered to another ruler without a fight. Actually, it was worse than that; he let the weaker vessel bear the brunt of temptation. If he secretly wanted to know what would happen when the fruit was eaten, then he was the ultimate coward by letting his wife find out for him rather than tasting it first himself.

There is a yearning in the heart of men and women for a certain quality of heroism in their relationships, and perhaps this is the source. What Adam and Eve failed to provide for each other in their moment of trial is what every man and woman secretly desires. We hear it in the great stories, the longing of a woman to see her man ride in and save the day just before she is overwhelmed by the villain. Why do women swoon when that happens and croon, "My hero!"?

Likewise, men long for a strong woman who will make them look good, not weak. What if Eve had asked the serpent, "Why are you questioning God?" What if she had turned to Adam and said, "Something's not right here. We shouldn't listen to this beast." Rarely are men attracted to the strong-willed woman who always demands her own way, but they admire the woman of noble character who maintains her femininity, honors her husband, yet can see to the heart of a situation and give her man the information he needs to act appropriately.

None of those heroic actions happened in Eden, and since then marriages have never been all that they were intended to be. We were made to be heroic, but we became cowards. And marriage has been characterized by cowardice every since.

The Core Problem

Why didn't Adam and Eve do the right thing? For me, the answer emerged when I recognized something about myself.

This recognition is not something I like to admit, but it gets to the heart of the marriage relationship and understanding why so many people aren't happy. Two personal examples should demonstrate what I mean. The first occurred on New Year's Eve, 1973, with a young woman I was dating. We had a lot of good times, freely laughing and kidding each other. Much of my kidding came in the form of put-downs. She would always laugh and either change the subject or fire some verbal barb back at me.

On this particular night, we took a walk in the southern California evening. It was unusually cool, and we bundled up against the nippy wind. During our conversation, I threw a sarcastic dart at her, and this time she was silent. After walking a couple of minutes, she stopped and forced me to look at her. "Al, I don't appreciate your put-downs. They aren't funny."

I was shocked. "But you've always laughed at them."

"I may have been laughing on the outside. But inside, I wonder why you say those things."

"I'm just kidding."

"Maybe. But they hurt. You've said you care about me, but when you say those things, it feels like you don't care about me at all. You're just going for a laugh at my expense. Which is the real you: the one who says he cares about me or the one who hurts me with put-downs?"

That night was the first time I truly confronted my real self, and I didn't like him. I realized that my sarcasm and put-downs were about making me look good at someone else's expense. That's deadly to any serious relationship. How could I take such an attitude into marriage? I realized I could not know what people were *really* feeling. They might be smiling because they were afraid to tell me what they really thought. I was better off being safe rather than cracking some pointed joke at someone else's expense. I'm extremely grateful that one woman was willing to teach me such a valuable lesson, and for the most part, I've tried to avoid humor at the expense of others ever since.

A second event occurred a few years ago when my wife and I had dinner with some friends. There were two single women at the event, and I spent a portion of that evening bantering with them, impressing them with what I thought were my clever intellect and humor. Later that evening, as my wife and I cuddled in bed, Jo observed, "You sure were full of yourself tonight."

To which I lovingly responded, "What else did you expect me to be full of?" Needless to say, I didn't get a very encouraging response to my smart-alecky comment. From my perspective, I was just entertaining some people, but Jo didn't see it that way. She saw her husband puffed up with himself, trying to show the world how great he was, and for her it was an ugly sight.

Jo's honesty forced me again to make an honest self-assessment. I discovered that when I thought more highly of myself than I should, I expected others to agree with that opinion. Fortunately, my wife revealed what they probably were really thinking: "What a jerk!"

This sad realization is, I believe, at the core of what went wrong in Eden. Adam and Eve weren't discerning or heroic because they were thinking about themselves rather than about God or about each other. The evidence for that is in their responses when God confronted them with their disobedience.

First, God asked Adam, who had just admitted he was afraid because he was naked: "Who told you that you were naked? Have you eaten from the tree that I commanded you not to eat from?"

This was a simple question requiring either a yes or a no. Adam didn't answer but rather passed blame to his wife: "The woman you put here with me—she gave me some fruit from the tree, and I ate it." In other words, it was Eve's fault! And by the way, God, You gave her to me. Adam was really saying, "God, it's Your fault that I ate of the fruit You told me not to eat."

God then turned His attention to Eve and asked, "What is this you have done?"

Eve admitted nothing. She, too, passed the blame: "The serpent deceived me, and I ate." Of course, there was a large element of truth in this statement—Eve had been deceived. But she accepted no responsibility. She could have sought help from Adam or God. Instead, she misplaced confidence in herself to handle the situation.

What was the problem here? The same problem I had: self-centeredness. When self is the center of our universe, it's hard to admit our weaknesses or faults.

The Problem with Self-Centeredness

Humans long for happiness. We generally attempt to attain it via self-centeredness and self-fulfillment. That's dangerous in a marriage. Self-centeredness may work as long as each person's needs happen to be met. But sooner or later, something inevitably happens to cause a conflict between my personal desires and those of my spouse.

When I face a situation with Jo where she wants me to do something I don't want to do, I have a choice: to do what I want because that's what I want, or to do what she needs done, even though I don't feel like doing it. Sometimes these are big issues, but usually it's the small events that cause tension.

Do I go to a kids' ball game when I would rather sit at home and read a book?

Do I clean up the kitchen on Sunday evening because I know

Jo hates facing a dirty kitchen on Monday morning, or do I resist, saying I deserve a break too?

Do I observe that the laundry needs moving along and do it for Jo, or do I just ignore it because that's her responsibility?

Every day there are situations that force me to confront my self-centered desires, and I must decide whether I will yield to my personal feelings or do what I perceive is the right thing. Of course, it helps if I work at perceiving. My wife rightly observes that I can be oblivious to certain needs. So, do I ask Jo if there's anything she'd like me to do for her on Saturday morning, or do I not ask because I have my plans and I don't want to risk her changing them? Plus, I'm not responsible for what I don't know. Right?

At the tree, Adam had to choose between doing what he knew was right or yielding to his curiosity and thus disobeying God. The former required courage. The latter meant doing what he felt like doing, because he thought it would make him happy.

The irony is that self-centeredness often produces the opposite of what we desire. I am actually the biggest obstacle to my own self-fulfillment. The more I concentrate on me—on my needs, my desires, my happiness—the less likely I am to find what I want. So I wonder, is happiness really the point of marriage? Or is it a by-product of something else in the relationship? My thoughts return to Jim and Bonnie. Jim said he wasn't happy. I suspect that Bonnie would have uttered the same complaint.

Happiness for Jim meant playing baseball and fulfilling his dream of pitching in the major leagues. It meant having an adoring wife who was his number-one fan. It meant Bonnie would never nag him about any of his deficiencies, which he didn't perceive anyway.

Happiness for Bonnie was finally settling down and having a place to call home. It was a husband who acted responsibly, recognized his family obligations, and got on with life by getting a real job. It was starting a family and raising children.

Neither Jim nor Bonnie was happy. Whose fault was that? Why, the other person's, of course!

That's the problem with the self-centered condition of humans. We view life from our perspective. When our partner doesn't see it the same way, we're frustrated.

Looking at the Options

So, what options did Jim have when he declared he was unhappy in his marriage? The same options we all have. First, Jim could follow through on his threat and divorce Bonnie. Apparently that is what happened a couple of years after our conversation in the parking lot. Let's think about that option.

If marriage really is about happiness, this is an obvious consideration. If I'm no longer happy with my spouse, then I leave. There's only one problem with that approach. How do I know if my spouse is *really* the reason I'm unhappy? Few seem to ask that question in the heat of divorce battles. But I was amazed to discover that, according to an analysis of the National Survey of Families and Households, "86 percent of unhappily married people who stick it out find that, five years later, their marriages are happier."[5] In fact, nearly 60 percent of those who rated their marriages as unhappy in the late 1980s, and who stayed married, rated the same marriage "very happy" or "quite happy" when reinterviewed five years later.[6] It appears that permanent unhappiness is rather rare in marriage!

There's one more point to consider with this option. If people divorce because they're unhappy, logically it should be expected that they would learn their lesson and find happiness the second time around. But the divorce rate is higher—60 percent—among second marriages.[7] There's simply no guarantee that an unhappy person will find permanent happiness with a different mate.

That leads to the second option: Just stick it out. For some

Christians, the fear of God and His commands causes them to make this their default button. God hates divorce. What God has joined together, let no man put apart. We'll stay together for the good of our children. The positive thing here is that, as we've seen, the chances are high that the marriage will improve. Marriage is a dynamic relationship that ebbs and flows among the good times and the not-so-good times.

Of course, there is a risk that things won't improve. That's certainly not motivating, and it begs the question again: Does God want me to remain miserable? Why would He order me to remain in an unhappy marriage?

An alternative in this scenario is simply to stay married because God says so, but man and wife go their separate ways in search of fulfillment and happiness. Husband and wife might remain cordial, but they sleep in different bedrooms and pursue personal fulfillment in their careers, separate hobbies, and friendships outside the marriage.

There is a third option. What if we had a reliable model for marriage that showed us what it was supposed to look like? For many centuries, the model for marriage existed in the home. Children, for better or worse, simply copied what they saw in their parents' marriages. Unfortunately, millions have lost any sense of what marriage should be because their parents divorced while they were growing up. What's worse, not only do many people not have a healthy model from their parents, but many claim they have never observed a good marriage up close. Judith Wallerstein observes in her landmark book *The Unexpected Legacy of Divorce*:

> Having been raised in divorced or very troubled homes [young adults] have no idea how to choose a partner or what to do to build the relationships. They regard their parents' divorce as a terrible failure and worry that they're doomed to follow in the

same footsteps.... Academic courses on marriage mostly look at families from the lofty perch of the family scholar and not from the perspective of children of divorce who feel "no one ever taught me."[8]

So, where does our culture look for role models? Celebrities, of course! I've often wondered why people are obsessed with tabloid newspapers screaming headlines about the latest pairings of movie stars, rock divas, and all-star athletes. Social critic Neal Gabler claims that our fixation on stories about celebrities transcends mere entertainment, that their personal journeys are narratives that guide our own relationships. Gabler observes that "entertainment is the primary standard of value for virtually everything in modern society.... To be a celebrity is widely regarded as the most exalted state of human existence."[9]

If this is true, what message are celebrities sending about marriage? While I was writing this portion of the book, the news media reported that actor Tom Cruise and actress Nicole Kidman were divorcing after 10 years of marriage. Why? According to one of their press releases, because of "difficulties inherent in divergent careers, which constantly keeps them apart." In other words, their individual acting careers were apparently more important than finding a way to make their marriage work for them and their two adopted children.

Celebrity news is full of who's going with whom and who's splitting up. Here are just a few news items I noted while writing this book. Actress Kim Basinger separated from actor-husband Alec Baldwin because of his problems with anger. Apparently Baldwin didn't have the patience to work through his problems in counseling. Tennis superstar Boris Becker was quoted as saying his divorce from German-American actress Barbara Feltus was the worst defeat he'd ever suffered. Becker said that his seven years of marriage "were the happiest of my life," yet that happiness didn't prevent him from starting a romance with a German rap singer who was once voted Germany's "most erotic woman." Actors Meg Ryan and Dennis Quaid seemed to their friends to have a happy marriage, but it ended when Meg fell for another superstar actor while filming a movie in Ecuador. Meanwhile, some celebs were opting out of marriage altogether. Goldie Hawn decided that, after two failed marriages, she preferred to say "I don't" while living with actor Kurt Russell.

The Perfect Role Model

I can only conclude that these beautiful people reveal little to us about true marital happiness. So, where do we look? Fortunately, God understood our need for a role model. In studying the Bible, I was surprised to discover that God didn't just give us instructions about marriage. He provided something far more significant: He infused marriage with meaning. While Jesus admitted that the law of Moses allowed for divorce in the case of infidelity, He said that from the beginning divorce was never God's intention. But He didn't just leave us to flounder, trying to make it work. He provided us with a picture of marriage, one that's both motivational and instructional. Perhaps it's not immediately evident to those who give the Bible a cursory reading, but it's clear as can be for those who are willing to examine the evidence.

Here are just a few examples from the Old Testament prophets:
"For your Maker is your husband."[10]

"'They broke my covenant, though I was a husband to them,' declares the LORD."[11]

"When I looked at you and saw that you were old enough for love, I spread the corner of my garment over you [culturally, this was a declaration of intention to marry] and covered your nakedness. I gave you my solemn oath and entered into a covenant with you, declares the Sovereign LORD, and you became mine."[12]

God showed us what marriage looks like because…

GOD, HIMSELF, GOT MARRIED!

As hard as we may try, we can't learn much more about the original marriage in Eden. The consequences of the Fall have so marred that picture that at best we get only a bare outline of God's intention. However, we can gaze at God's marriage and discover His heart. It is from this artistic masterpiece that we gain the objective perspective we need for our marriages.

So let's move in a new direction and examine when and how God got married, what His marriage is like, and how His marriage points us in the right direction for our own relationship with our spouse.

6

God's Betrothal

*If God really did get married, the logical question is, when? I had to
go back to Genesis, and when I found what I thought was the answer,
I again tried to see this from the viewpoint of the two angels whom
we met in chapter two. What follows is the first of five frescoes,
showing various facets of God's marriage.*

After the cataclysmic flood that wiped out all but eight humans,
there was little for the angels to observe on planet Earth. For a time,
God seemed to have lost any emotional attachment to His creation.
Once, the Creator became alarmed when the people attempted to
build a tower to the heavens. He stepped into that situation and
confused their language, thus effectively scattering them to various
parts of the world.

Abdiel and Zephon faithfully served their Master, content to
exist in His presence and to do His bidding. Then Zephon came
running one day and called to his friend, "Come with me, quick.
You've got to see this!"

They hurried to the stadium where the heavenly throngs had

watched the Master sculpt His masterpiece. The crowd was smaller now, but a murmur of surprise and anticipation buzzed among the angels. The Creator was talking to a man.

"Who is that?" asked Abdiel.

"The man's name is Abram," Zephon answered. "Listen!"

The Creator was talking to Abram as a friend, the way He'd talked to Adam in the garden but rarely to anyone else since. "Leave your country, your people, and your father's household and go to the land I will show you," said the Lord.[1]

The angels saw the man respond but couldn't hear the words. They clearly heard their Master reply: "I will make you into a great nation and I will bless you; I will make your name great, and you will be a blessing. I will bless those who bless you, and whoever curses you I will curse; and all peoples on earth will be blessed through you."

When the two parted, the angels watched as Abram gathered his wife, his nephew, Lot, and his servants. They packed all their belongings on camels, gathered their livestock, and headed toward another country.

"Where are they going?" Abdiel said.

"I have no idea." So they watched and observed as Abram arrived in the land of Canaan. The angels followed this man closely, observing how the Creator appeared to him at Shechem, and how he built an altar to the Lord. Later, Abram and his entourage escaped from famine into Egypt. They observed his return to Canaan a much richer man with many livestock, and they watched as Abram and his nephew divided the land, with Lot taking the more fertile region in the Jordan Valley for himself.

Again the Creator met with Abram. Again the angels heard Him speak: "Lift up your eyes from where you are and look north and south, east and west. All the land that you see I will give to you and your offspring forever. I will make your offspring like the dust of

the earth, so that if anyone could count the dust, then your offspring could be counted." Then, with what seemed like a clap on
the shoulder, as a proud father might speak to his son, God said,
"Go, walk through the length and breadth of the land, for I am giving it to you."

"I haven't seen Him so excited in ages," said Abdiel.

Zephon smiled as he reflected. "This is different from when He
walked with Enoch. Or when He instructed Noah to build the ark.
This is the kind of warmth we saw only with the original couple."

"I wonder, why does He want to give this man this particular
tract of land? He has never done this before. People have simply
settled on the land they wanted—there was always plenty to go
around."

"If the humans continue to grow in numbers, someday there
will be much less land available. But you are right in observing that
this is highly unusual. Why this man? And why this piece of land?"

And so the angels continued to observe. The man and the Creator met occasionally, always at the latter's discretion. One visitation was in a vision that terrified the man until God calmed him,
saying, "Do not be afraid, Abram. I am your shield, your very great
reward."

"Our Master is restraining Himself with the creature," Zephon
observed. "We are used to seeing Him in His glory, but the creature
is scared at the least glimpse—"

"Look!" Abdiel interrupted. "They are talking as friends. The
man has become bolder."

They listened as Abram expressed his frustration: "O Sovereign
Lord, what can you give me since I remain childless? You have
given me no children; so a servant in my household will be my
heir."

"This man will not be your heir," the Creator answered, "but a
son coming from your own body will be your heir." Then He led

Abram from the tent where they had been talking. It was the dead of night, and the fires had died down to only a few embers. No one stirred in the tents of the servants. A camel grunted as they walked by, out of the camp and into the desert. No moon was shining, no breeze stirred. They stood in absolute silence some distance outside the camp. "Look up at the heavens," said the Creator.

The pair stared into the sky. The great ribbon of the galaxy swept across the blackness, blazing in its glory. "Count the stars— if indeed you can count them."

Abram nearly laughed. It was absurd to think he could number the stars.

"So shall your offspring be." The Lord's words were clear, definitive.

Abram nodded his head, and even in the dim light of the stars, the angels could see the hint of a smile passing over his face. "I believe You," Abram said.

The Creator then drew Abram's attention to the land surrounding them. As the light began to shine in the east, He said, "I am the Lord, who brought you out of Ur of the Chaldeans to give you this land to take possession of it."

Abram still didn't own any of the land God had promised him. There were other tribes, Canaanites and Perizzites, living there. So Abram asked the logical question, "O Sovereign Lord, how can I know that I will gain possession of it?"

In answer, God ordered Abram, "Bring me a heifer, a goat and a ram, each three years old, along with a dove and young pigeon." Abram understood the instructions, and at daybreak he proceeded to gather the animals and lead them into the desert. Early in the afternoon, he slaughtered the three larger animals and divided them in half, placing the halves opposite each other. The birds he kept intact.

"What is he doing?" Abdiel asked.

"Abram and our Master are making a covenant," Zephon answered. "I've observed this on a number of occasions. It usually occurs when two tribes make a treaty, or when a boy and a girl are promised for marriage to each other by their families. When everything is ready, usually at sundown, the two parties to the agreement—the fathers or tribal leaders—walk barefoot through the blood of the separated animals, thereby signifying that this is what will happen to either of them if they fail to keep their end of the bargain."

"In other words, if one of them breaks the promise, he forfeits his life."

"That's correct."

"But God never breaks His promises. Why is this necessary?"

"I imagine that the man doesn't know God the way we do."

While Abram waited for God to arrive at the meeting place, vultures began to attack the carrion. Abram shooed them away. Then, as the sun was setting, Abram fell asleep, and a terrible darkness descended. The two angels were engrossed, barely aware that the heavenly stadium had filled completely to observe the scene. They heard their Lord speak to Abram, explaining that Abram's descendants would surely own this land, but not for another 400 years. "You, however, will go to your fathers in peace and be buried at a good old age. In the fourth generation, your descendants will come back here."

The sun had now completely set and it was pitch-black—the angels couldn't even see stars. Then, through the darkness, the angels saw a light, like a smoking firepot with a blazing torch, pass between the pieces of carcass. Meanwhile, Abram remained in a deep sleep. "That's most unusual," said Zephon.

"Why? What's wrong?" asked Abdiel.

"As I explained earlier, when two individuals make a covenant, they both pass between the pieces of the sacrificed animals, signifying that both accept the terms of the agreement and will pay with their lives if they violate any of the conditions. But in this case, only God Himself passed through."

"So only He is liable, right? And He can't break His word."

"You don't understand. Both the man and God are bound by this agreement. But God is liable if either party violates the contract. If the man or any of his descendants breaks his part of the agreement, God must pay the price for the man's breach."

"That doesn't make any sense."

Zephon was quiet for a moment, meditating on what he'd just witnessed. "I wonder," he finally said. "I think God is saying He cares so much for the man that He is willing to do whatever is necessary to make this relationship work."

"Even die!" Abdiel was horrified by what he'd just said and slapped his hand over his mouth.

Zephon nodded his head in agreement with his fellow angel. "You're right. This makes no sense. No sense at all."

7

The Covenant Marriage

The ceremony the angels witnessed was a solemn occasion, used only for the most important decisions, including marriage. In a covenant sealed with blood, the father of the groom and the father of the bride each slit the throat of an animal—a sheep, goat, or heifer—and drained the blood onto the ground. Then they walked barefoot in the blood between the pieces of carcass, saying by their actions, "May I pay with my life if this covenant is broken."[1]

Technically, Abram and his descendants weren't married to God in the same sense that we understand a wedding ceremony today. It would be more accurate to say they were betrothed, which means that they were promised to each other. It is the same for Christ and His bride, the church. The wedding feast celebrating this marriage remains in the future at the wedding supper of the Lamb.[2]

In our culture, couples are first engaged—they declare their intent to marry—but either party may back out before the wedding day, and there is no legal consequence for breaking an engagement. Such was not the case with betrothal. A betrothal was an ironclad contract that could be severed only by unfaithfulness or death.

Though a couple might not celebrate and consummate their marriage for years, legally they were still considered married.

This was the case with Joseph and Mary when she was found with child by the Holy Spirit—they were promised to each other even though their marriage hadn't been consummated. Society viewed them as married. If a girl who was betrothed was found not to be a virgin before the wedding feast, when the marriage would be consummated, she could be executed.[3] This explains why Joseph, upon hearing that Mary was pregnant, decided not to make a public spectacle of his wife but to put her away privately—that is, until God spoke to him and revealed the identity of the child in her womb.[4]

I wonder what the impact was on the children who witnessed a covenant sealed in blood by their fathers. Though they might hardly know each other, and indeed it might be years before they were ready to celebrate the wedding, they surely understood the commitment being made. There was only one way to escape from this marriage—by death.

The Real Cost of a Wedding

When a couple marries today, a lot of effort goes into the wedding. Adding up the costs of a wedding dress, tuxedos, dresses for the bridesmaids, rings, invitations, flowers, music, photographer, wedding cake, and reception, the average couple spends nearly $30,000.[5]

When we were married, Jo was a poor schoolteacher and I was a poor writer. We had less than $1,000 for our wedding. Jo brilliantly maximized the reach of our limited budget by making her own wedding dress and soliciting help from friends and family for such things as food preparation.

A major element of our planning was the ceremony itself. We'd both attended many weddings, and the norm of the late seventies was for each couple to custom-design their ceremony. One beautiful church wedding I attended lasted less than ten minutes. After a very brief reception, the couple rushed off on their honeymoon. I attended a hippie wedding in a park south of San Francisco where the ceremony consisted of everyone who wished getting up and imparting some piece of wisdom they'd learned about marriage. The couple then pledged to remain faithful to each other as long as they both loved each other, and a minister declared them married. It was a nice gathering, but somehow unsatisfying.

The norm for most couples was to write their own vows. In that spirit, Jo and I sat down one Sunday afternoon to write out our commitment to each other. We discussed what we were doing in marriage: pledging to be faithful, to take care of each other, to support one another during good times and hard times. We scribbled several drafts, but none of them captured the right tone.

Finally, we settled on the following:

"I, Al, take thee, Jo, to be my lawfully wedded wife, to have and to hold from this day forward, for better or for worse, for richer or for poorer, in sickness and in health 'til death do us part."

"I, Jo, take thee, Al, to be my lawfully wedded husband, to have and to hold from this day forward, for better or for worse, for richer or for poorer, in sickness and in health 'til death do us part."

Those words, or a slight variation of them, had served Christians for centuries, and we couldn't find anything that better expressed what we were committing to each other. For us, they expressed the vows we were making—an irrevocable commitment to each other with God as our witness.

We also decided that because we wanted to dedicate our marriage to God, our first act as a married couple would be to partake in Holy Communion. It was our way of saying that we were being united together in Christ.

What Happens in a Wedding?

While Jo and I carefully planned the ceremony, like most couples we were also in a bit of a daze during the service. I imagine Jim and Bonnie felt the same way when they had their beautiful church wedding in the early seventies. In retrospect, I needed to understand what we had done. Was our wedding really a covenant, or was it simply a legal procedure? A covenant sounds so final, so uncompromising. Just what did this mean, and why do it this way instead of just writing a simple contract or appearing before a justice of the peace or simply living together?

To answer that, I compared our church wedding service to the ceremony between God and Abram. Abram was an ordinary human being approached by the almighty God, who said, in so many words, that He loved His creation. I wonder what Abram felt about those first encounters. Out of the blue, God approaches him and asks him to leave his country, his "gods," his people, his father's household, and go to a land "I will show you."[6] God must have made it very attractive. What man could resist the chance to become a great nation and to be a blessing to the entire world? All God asked was that Abram make Him the one and only object of his worship.

When a man and woman marry, they leave their parents and form a new home. So Abram left his home and family and traveled to a new land.

A wife usually takes a new name when she is married. Abram was given a new name: Abraham.

A husband and wife exchange rings as a symbol of their union. Abram was given a symbol of the union with God—circumcision.

The children of a married couple inherit the property of their parents. Likewise, the equivalent of a will was provided so that Abraham's children would inherit the land.

An important point to remember is that Abram had a choice: He didn't have to go. Love can be offered, but it can't be demanded. Even after Abram left Ur, there were plenty of uncertain moments and unanswered questions. God commended him for his great faith—he believed God. Still, eventually it had to come down to this point: I believe You, but how can I know for sure that You really will do all You say You will do?

Jim and I and millions of other people have faced the same challenge. Bonnie surely heard Jim say that he loved her, but how could she know with all of her being that he really did love her, that this wasn't some temporary rush of emotion, that he wouldn't find someone else more desirable someday and abandon her? If she didn't ask those questions, she should have. Today, that is the terrible risk many people feel, the reason they hesitate to get married. Like millions of people, Bonnie had experienced firsthand the pain of her parents' divorce. If her parents had failed in their marriage, how could she be sure she would do any better? Unfortunately, her worst fears came true.

Judith Wallerstein, in her 25-year study of the effects of divorce, observed: "Men and women from divorced families live in fear that they will repeat their parents' history, hardly daring to hope that they can do better.... As children grow up and choose partners of their own, they lack this central image of the intact marriage. In its place they confront a void that threatens to swallow them whole.... Their conclusion is simple....*Failure is inevitable.*"[7]

Failure is not inevitable, but for many married couples today, there is a back door for escape called divorce. It is important to bolt that door shut. For God and Abraham, the covenant eliminated the possibility of divorce. Today most people don't understand what covenant means. Our culture is built on contracts, and everyone knows that a crackerjack lawyer can find a loophole if you really want out. So contracts get longer and longer as the parties try to

68   your
m a r r i a g e
masterpiece

close all possible loopholes, but litigation increases because people change their minds and want release from their agreements.

Is It Just a Piece of Paper?

Today couples get a marriage license when they marry. But with no-fault divorce laws, that license can be nullified at any time for any reason or no reason at all. No wonder many couples conclude that they needn't bother with a piece of paper or with a contract or a ceremony of any kind. Why not just move into the same home and live together? Millions of couples are choosing this option. Later some close the deal with marriage, though these marriages face a higher chance of divorce than those of couples who never cohabitated.[8]

For couples who do marry, many negotiate a contract prior to the wedding ceremony. These prenuptial agreements spell out each person's rights and property, the division of expenses and household chores, rules on sexual exclusivity, and how property will be divided if, or when, the marriage dissolves.

A covenant is not at all like a prenuptial agreement. For one thing, there is no escape clause. In ancient times, a covenant was a legal agreement, but with two major differences from contracts today. A covenant was made before deity. And the penalty for breaking it was death. People might negotiate out of contracts, but not out of a covenant.

The covenant between God and Abraham was more binding than a wedding certificate is today. God impressed on Abraham the importance of the covenant: "As for you, you must keep my covenant, you and your descendants after you." While Abraham didn't walk the blood path, there was a symbol of his acceptance of the agreement. The proof of Abraham's commitment was that he and every male descendant was circumcised.[9]

But in the covenant of blood, God traveled the blood path

alone. By doing so, he said that if Abraham or any of his descendants violated this contract, God would pay the price with His own blood. There would come a day when God would heroically have to keep that promise.

How the Church Has Viewed Weddings

For centuries, in liturgical churches, the service of holy matrimony has been clearly spelled out word for word. As I read several liturgies, I was struck by the similarities between the church service of holy matrimony and the biblical concept of covenant.

For example, the marriage service is conducted before God. Historically, a covenant was always a religious ceremony, made before God or gods as witnesses. It was the one treaty between enemies that was enforceable, because neither party was willing to risk the wrath of their deity.

In the English *Book of Common Prayer* (1662), a wedding service begins with the minister addressing the congregation: "Dearly beloved, we are gathered together here *in the sight of God*...to join together this man and this woman in holy Matrimony."[10] Again and again, the couple and witnesses are reminded that God is witness to this union.

Second, a covenant had witnesses. Likewise, the marriage vows are made before human witnesses. Why is that important? A pastor I know challenged a friend who had just announced he was leaving his wife of six years. "Oh, no, you're not!" said the pastor. "You made a vow to love your wife until death. I know. I was there and I heard you. Now you stay with her and work things out." The man was shocked, but he stayed, and today their marriage is much healthier. I wonder what would happen if, like this pastor, more witnesses challenged couples to fulfill their wedding vows.

Third, both a covenant and a traditional marriage ceremony

70   your
m a r r i a g e
masterpiece

declared the seriousness of the commitment. In the *Book of Common Prayer*, the minister utters these words in his opening exhortation to the congregation and the couple standing before him: "Holy Matrimony...is commended of Saint Paul to be honourable among all men; and therefore is not by any to be enterprised... unadvisedly, lightly, or wantonly, to satisfy men's carnal lusts and appetites, like brute beasts that have no understanding; but reverently, discreetly, advisedly, soberly, and in the fear of God."[11]

Recently, as I reflected on the vows Jo and I exchanged at our wedding, I was struck by the one-sidedness of our commitment. There were no qualifiers or disclaimers. I had promised to love Jo for better or worse until death, regardless of her actions or attitude. Likewise, Jo promised to have me for richer or poorer, in sickness and health, for as long as we both should live, regardless of how well or poorly I behaved. No doubt we both assumed we would reciprocate in our love for each other. However, our vows said nothing about being loved back. By our words, each of us assumed 100 percent responsibility for the marriage. That's the nature of covenant. Each party makes an irrevocable vow.

Fourth, something of great value was exchanged. God wanted to give Abraham and his descendants a country, but He did it in the context of family. Did Abraham realize he was actually getting the better end of the deal? He was entering into a long-term relationship with the God of the universe. The land was very important, but it wasn't the most important thing—it was a symbol of the value of their relationship.

I am impressed again by the nature of the exchange in the traditional marriage service. It particularly struck me when I read the words uttered by the husband when he places the wedding ring on his wife's finger: "With this ring I thee wed, with my body I thee worship, and with all my worldly goods I thee endow."[12] In other words, the husband gave everything he had to his wife, including his body and his earthly possessions. No longer were there his or her possessions. Everything was theirs. Why is this important? Because in giving our all, we actually gain what we want.

You Gain by Giving

Writer Patricia McGerr tells the story of a man named Johnny Lingo who lived on an island in the South Pacific. Johnny was a wealthy trader, respected for his ability to strike a hard bargain. Except when it came to securing his wife. In these islands, a man bought his wife from her father by paying from one to six cows. Two or three cows would buy a fair-to-middling wife; four or five, a highly satisfactory one.

Johnny wanted to marry Sarita, a plain woman who lived on the island of Kiniwata and was scared of her own shadow. For her, Johnny offered the unheard-of sum of eight cows. The residents of Kiniwata smirked that such a successful businessman could pay such an outrageous price. They figured he was a sucker when it came to love.

The author decided to find out more about Johnny and his wife, so she sailed to the nearby island where Johnny lived and called on his home. When she met his wife, she was amazed to find the most beautiful woman she'd ever seen. When Patricia inquired about what happened, Johnny explained, "Do you ever think what it must mean to a woman to know that her husband has settled on the lowest price for which she can be bought? And then later, when the women talk, they boast of what their husbands paid for them. One says four cows, another maybe six. How does she feel, the woman who was sold for one or two? This could not happen to my Sarita."

"Then you did this just to make your wife happy?" asked Patricia.

"I wanted Sarita to be happy, yes. But I wanted more than that.

You say she is different. This is true. Many things can change a woman…. But the thing that matters most is what she thinks about herself. In Kiniwata, Sarita believed she was worth nothing. Now she knows she is worth more than any other woman in the islands."[13]

What doesn't cost much doesn't mean much. To His bride, God initially gave a piece of property. But a day would come when God would pay a far higher price to prove His love.

There is one more observation about covenants. There was no escape mechanism. There could be blessings and curses listed—and God spelled those out when the covenant with Abraham's descendants was renewed on Mount Sinai. But the covenant itself could not be revoked by God or by Abraham or by his descendants. That's the same concept I found in a traditional marriage ceremony. When Jo and I married, there was no escape clause. Society and its laws might recognize our right to divorce if we so choose. But Jo and I decided that our vows before God didn't give us that option. We were committed to each other through thick and thin.

Obviously, Jim and millions of others feel that such permanence fences them in. But Jo and I feel secure within these boundaries. Without the possibility of divorce, Jo and I know that, regardless of our problems, we will be there for each other. And when we disagree or fight, we had better figure out a way to resolve our differences, for we are going to be together for a very long time.

It's interesting that even governmental institutions have started to recognize the benefit of covenant relationships. In 1997, Louisiana was the first state to offer couples two marriage options: a typical license under no-fault divorce laws, and a covenant marriage that allowed for divorce only on limited grounds and only after a waiting period of one year.

Dr. Steven Nock, a professor of sociology at the University of Virginia, believes the dynamics of a relationship change under a covenant:

For standard couples, the major factor that attracted them to their partner and to marriage was the fact that they were in love with each other. Covenant couples offer a lot more explanation as to why they got married: compatibility, relatives, sharing common values, the likelihood of being able to raise children successfully—the mundane and prosaic aspects of life. But [for] the standard couples…when they get married, they're in love and that's about the beginning and the end of it.[14]

It's So One-Sided

Because of the seriousness Jo and I share about our marriage, I have always felt extremely uncomfortable when I see couples trivialize their marriage vows. Shortly after we were married, a popular new show started airing on weekend nights. Called *The Love Boat*, it featured three couples on a cruise ship and followed their romantic adventures from boarding to debarking a few days later. We usually watched the show in bed, relaxing after a busy workweek. We enjoyed the characters and the story lines that seemed to emphasize genuine love.

But soon, the show's stories began to change. By the second season, married couples were coming on board looking for love in all the wrong places. I became increasingly frustrated by the implied infidelity, and finally, one evening, during a commercial break, I jumped out of bed and shut off the television. We never watched the show again.

Ever since, when a show, novel, or movie features married people in adulterous relationships, I nearly always cut it off. Perhaps I could stomach such stories if they also showed the real consequences of adultery, but that is rarely the case. In fact, nonmarital sex has become more and more glorified over the years, to the point that when one does see a healthy marriage relationship in a story, it's shocking because it's so unusual.

For me, what's troubling is the ease with which marriage vows are ignored or abandoned. When God made His vows to Abraham, they were ironclad. Marriage liturgies in the church never mention the possibility of breach. And Jesus Himself said that it was never God's intention that a husband and wife would divorce. "What God has joined together, let man not separate."[15]

One verse in the book of Deuteronomy captures the seriousness of the marriage covenant. Moses exhorted the Israelites before they entered the Promised Land: "Whatever your lips utter you must be sure to do, because you made your vow freely to the Lord your God with your own mouth."[16]

My conclusion is that we need to view the wedding ceremony far more seriously than we have. When a man and woman stand before the minister, they are standing before God, and when they make their vows to each other, they are also making them to God, who will hold us accountable for what we promise. Based on that, we should commit that the word "divorce" will never be uttered with regard to our marriages, for divorce is simply not an option.

I have also concluded that marriage is intended to be the human relationship that reflects how committed God is to us. When God walked the blood path in covenant with Abraham, He committed Himself regardless of how well or poorly Abraham performed his part. History proves that God kept His commitment—and if anyone had reason to divorce, it was God.

One thing troubles me about this discussion. Within the covenant, there seems to be an absence of romance. Isn't that a critical element in the happiness of any marriage? If God got married, was there any romantic passion between Him and the people of Israel? The answer from Scripture is very clear. Our second vignette of God's marriage is His love story. It begins where all love stories start, with the first meeting between a boy and a girl.

8

The Greatest Love Story of All Time

Certain love stories—like Cinderella, Snow White, and Beauty and the Beast—have stood the test of time. People read these books and watch the movie or play versions over and over because they are so satisfying. The story that follows is, I believe, the inspiration for every great love story ever written.

Once upon a time, in the region of Lebanon in the Middle East, there lived a girl named Cindy. Her family grew grapes and raised sheep and goats. Unfortunately, the father had passed away by the time this story begins, and Cindy's lazy brothers were running the farm.

Under the hot sun, Cindy was pruning grapevines. "You're not working hard enough!" shouted one of her brothers. His siblings laughed and took another gulp of wine in a shady grove, passing the wineskin among themselves.

76   your
m a r r i a g e
masterpiece

"Yeah," said another brother as he wiped his mouth on his sleeve, "you still need to water the goats."

"Nice suntan!" joked a third brother. "All the girls must be jealous!" The young men laughed uncontrollably.

Cindy turned away so her brothers wouldn't see her tears, which would only cause them to increase their merciless teasing. It was like this day after day. She did all the work while her brothers sat around drinking wine. She longed to confide to her mother, but the mother was frail, and anyway, her oldest brother always managed to spin a satisfactory explanation.

One day her brothers went off to town to party with friends. Cindy diligently worked in the vineyards, trimming some branches, lifting limbs from the ground so they wouldn't rot in the rain or be eaten by animals. She was tempted to sit and rest, but there was much work to do, and she simply couldn't let her mother down—the family depended on the revenue from these grapes.

Suddenly, Cindy noticed a young man staring at her from a knoll just beyond the vineyard. She kept working, hoping he would leave—she was uncomfortable with his stares. But he didn't leave. She could see he was studying her, with a big grin on his face. So she stopped working and stared back.

The young man stood and announced, "The young lily has noticed me."

"Who, me?" Cindy had been called many names, none of them a flower.

"Yes, you are a lily among thorns!"

Cindy had to laugh at the young man's brashness. "Me! I've spent too much time in the sun. I'm darker than any of the girls in this area."

The young man bounded down toward her as he said, "Ah, you are the most beautiful woman I've ever laid eyes on. Let me take a closer look." He stopped in front of her and nodded his head as he gently said, "Yes, you are a hard worker. Yet you are the most delicate and beautiful of roses. Your eyes are gentle like doves."

Cindy blushed, then laughed. "My, my. You sure are sweet with words. Who are you? I've never seen you around here before."

"You haven't! I'm shocked. Surely you must know who I am!"

Cindy shook her head. "No, I'm sure I would have recognized you. What is your name?"

"Let's just say I'm a shepherd lad."

He said it in such a winsome way that she could only laugh and play along. "Okay, shepherd lad. Where are your sheep?"

"Oh, they're all around. Can't you see them?"

"You're teasing me. I don't see any sheep."

"You don't? Well, they are around. I have lots and lots of sheep."

The young woman blushed again, and the young man backed away. "I'll be back," he said. "Can I find you here tomorrow? About this time?"

"Oh, yes. I'm not going anywhere. My work keeps me chained to this vineyard."

"Then tomorrow it is!" And quickly the young man scampered over the knoll and disappeared.

True to his word, the young man returned the next day, and the day after, and in no time Cindy was madly in love. One afternoon, the shepherd boy helped her finish her work by gathering the goats and filling the water trough. The animals seemed comfortable with this man. Then he said, "I have a surprise." He led her over the knoll, and there, in a grove by the stream, was a beautiful meal spread out for them. It was some of the finest food she'd ever tasted. For a moment she wondered how a shepherd boy was able to prepare such a magnificent meal.

During that dinner, the shepherd proposed. "May I speak to your father about us?" he said, indicating the desire to negotiate a marriage arrangement.

"My father is dead," Cindy answered.

"May I speak to your mother, then?"

"I'm afraid my brothers will have more say in this matter. They won't want to lose my labor."

"I see." The shepherd had a sly grin. "I think I know how to handle them. Just leave it all to me."

Cindy was skeptical, but she loved him so much. If anyone could handle her brothers, this man could.

"I have to go away for a while," he said. "Will you wait for me?"

"Of course, I will wait." Her heart leaped at the thought of living with this simple peasant man, yet she also ached at the thought of waiting. "Please, don't be too long. I don't think I can stand being separated from you."

"I will be back soon. Until then, I will think only of your lovely face. And hear in my heart your sweet voice." Quickly, without a heartrending good-bye, he was off.

How significantly Cindy's life had changed! One day she was simply a laborer in the fields; the next, an engaged woman anticipating an escape from the tyranny of her brothers. Of course, she still labored, but she knew it would not last much longer, for her lover, a rugged, handsome shepherd, was coming back for her. All her thoughts dwelt on how happy they would be together.

Then her heart lurched. She didn't even know his name! If he was but a shepherd, how could he afford the bride price? Her brothers would certainly drive a hard bargain. Where would this man get the money to buy her freedom?

How love overcomes such obstacles! Her lover seemed so confident. He must have options. She would trust him to find a way to pay the money.

Weeks passed. Cindy's mother and brothers said nothing about any marriage arrangement. The brothers only demanded more work out of her. She wondered: Had the shepherd talked to them? Had an agreement been negotiated? There was no word.

Every thought of Cindy's was for her love. How she missed him! How she longed for his return! She dreamed of him—sweet dreams of their courtship, of his poetic words of affection, of the love they would share as husband and wife.

Occasionally the dreams turned dark. One night, she dreamed that she was searching for her love and couldn't find him. She was in a large city, at night. She was running up and down the streets and alleys, calling for him. Windows opened and angry voices called for her to shut up. A group of young men found her, and she begged them for news of her love. They laughed at her, stole her robe, and beat her, leaving her writhing in the street. Then she awoke in a sweat-soaked bed in her humble country home. She could hear her mother tossing fitfully in the next room, and her brothers in another room, snoring loudly in their wine-induced stupor.

Weeks and months passed. Doubts increasingly invaded her thoughts. The shepherd boy had forgotten her. He'd found another and decided not to marry her after all. He couldn't meet the bride price and didn't have the heart to tell her there would be no wedding. But she banished all such thoughts, for she had gazed into his eyes and seen true love. Deep in her heart, she knew he had to return.

One day, as Cindy labored in the vineyard, she heard a shout from the neighboring field. She looked up toward the desert and saw a column of dust and smoke, announcing the arrival of a large caravan. "The king is coming! The king is coming!" went the shouts.

A neighbor girl ran over to tell Cindy the news. "My brother saw him!" she said breathlessly. "There are sixty soldiers escorting him. And camels and horses. He's in this beautiful cedar carriage—with a gold base and posts of silver, and it has purple upholstery perfumed with incense. Come! Let's go see! Did I tell you, the king is wearing his crown? This is so exciting!"

The girl pulled on Cindy's arm, and they ran to the road to watch the entourage enter the village. The sun caught the shields of the first row of soldiers. Cindy shuddered as she noted the swords at their sides. These were fierce-looking men who could surely protect their king. They passed by her, two by two. Then she heard a command to halt, and the royal carriage stopped right in front of her!

A face popped out of the window, and with a sly smile, the king looked right into Cindy's eyes and said, "How beautiful you are, my darling! Oh, how beautiful! Like a lily among thorns is my darling among the maidens."

Cindy's heart jumped at the voice—the voice of the shepherd, her lover! The king nimbly stepped out of the carriage and faced her. Gently, he grasped her shoulders and looked her over. "Arise, my darling, my beautiful one, and come with me."

The next hours were a blur. There were lavish gifts for her and her family. Cindy was dressed in the finest linen for the trip to the capital and the king's palace. The celebration was greater than any dream she could have imagined. There were courtiers, noblemen, ladies to meet her every need, and singers to entertain them. "We rejoice and delight in you," they sang. "We will praise your love more than wine."

A special song was commissioned for the occasion. Cindy's heart stirred as she heard these words sung:

Listen, O daughter, consider and give ear;
Forget your people and your father's house.
The king is enthralled by your beauty;

Honor him, for he is your lord.
Your sons will take the place of your fathers;
You will make them princes throughout the land.

She had to keep pinching herself to tell herself this wasn't a dream. Never could she have imagined such joy. Then the party was over and the two of them were alone in the king's chambers. Tenderly, the king said, "Your lips are like a scarlet ribbon; your mouth is lovely." She blushed while savoring his words. "You have stolen my heart, my bride; you have stolen my heart with one glance of your eyes." Then he put a necklace around her neck. "You are a garden locked up, my bride; you are a spring enclosed, a sealed fountain."

If this was a dream, Cindy didn't wake up. Poetry poured from her lips: "Awake, north wind, and come, south wind! Blow on my garden, that its fragrance may spread abroad. Let my lover come into his garden and taste its choice fruits." With those words, the king blew out the candle and led her to his bed.

And they lived happily ever after!

Their love affair rarely waned. The couple was madly in love, and only the finest poetry could begin to express their passion. However, Cindy couldn't forget her home. As comfortable as she was in a palace, she missed the earth, the fields, the smell of the blossoms when they opened on the vines. The king had purchased the vineyard of Cindy's youth, and caretakers were hired to work the fields. Now she wanted to go back to her vineyard to see the place where the shepherd-king had found her.

"Come, my lover," she said one day. "Let us go to the vineyards to see if the vines have budded, if their blossoms have opened. There I will give you my love."

"Why, aren't you happy here in the palace with me?" the king asked gently.

"I belong to you, my lover, and your desire is for me," she

replied. "Come, let's go to the countryside. Let's get out of this castle and spend the night in the villages. Let us go early to the vineyards to see if the vines have budded, if their blossoms have opened, and if the pomegranates are in bloom." Then she lowered her eyes and coyly repeated, "There I will give you my love."

The king couldn't resist. With a huge entourage, the couple returned to the site of their engagement. Soldiers sealed the perimeter so they could have absolute privacy. Husband and wife cuddled on the lush grass—Cindy loved the way the king put his left arm under her head and wrapped his strong right arm around her. In the distance, they heard a chorus singing, while in privacy the king and his beloved again expressed their undying love for each other.

Sighing contentedly in his embrace, Cindy said, "Place me like a seal over your heart, like a seal on your arm; for love is as strong as death, its jealousy unyielding as the grave. It burns like blazing fire, like a mighty flame. Many waters cannot quench love; rivers cannot wash it away."

9

The Passionate Marriage

Love stories have a common plot. Boy meets girl. He begins to pursue her, but obstacles prevent their coming together. Sometimes the girl doesn't like the boy, and he has to overcome various challenges to win her affections. Ultimately love triumphs, the couple is married, and they live happily ever after.

I believe that we never tire of this scheme because, whether we acknowledge it or not, it reflects our yearning for intimacy with one special individual. The story in chapter eight is more than 3,000 years old. It is the drama behind the poetry in the Song of Songs—the story of how King Solomon discovered a beautiful woman and fell in love with her.[1] I chose the name of Cindy because we don't know the name of the Shulamite woman (and because it sounds a little like "Cinderella," the name of the heroine in a story that could have been inspired by the Song of Solomon).

Commentators recognize that the Song of Songs is also God's story.

God is a romantic! He wanted a lover, and He passionately pursued her.

I don't recall hearing that concept while growing up in church.

84   your
m a r r i a g e
masterpiece

I'd heard or read many thinkers express their picture of God. Some portrayed Him as a mighty dictator, looking over all we did and passing judgment. Others saw Him as a kind grandfather who patted us on the head, told us to be good, and sent us on our way. Some viewed Him as a shepherd who has His hands full herding us, His unruly sheep. Still others—often people hurt and bitter about life—viewed Him as an uncaring Creator who made this world and placed us in it, then totally detached Himself and let whatever happened happen.

There was truth in some of those images. God is a king; He is a father; He is a shepherd. But a passionate lover? A suitor who felt tender affection for His creation, jealousy when we wandered away from Him, or anger when we chose to place other things higher than Him? That didn't seem like the God whose story was portrayed on stained-glass windows in the churches I attended.

God Reveals His Heart

Something powerful drew me to this image of God the romantic. Of course, I'd read in Ephesians about the church being the bride of Christ. But I viewed that more as a metaphor. Surely this didn't mean God felt powerful emotions toward us. Or did He? I reread the Bible in an attempt to clarify my understanding of God, and I was astonished to find passages where God spoke like a man hopelessly smitten:

"I am now going to allure her; I will lead her into the desert and speak tenderly to her."[2]

"I remember the devotion of your youth, how as a bride you loved me and followed me through the desert."[3]

"How can I give you up? … My heart is changed within me; all my compassion is aroused."[4]

"Can a mother forget the baby at her breast and have no compassion on the child she has borne? Though she may forget, I will not forget you! See, I have engraved you on the palms of my hands."[5]

"Though the mountains be shaken and the hills be removed, yet my unfailing love for you will not be shaken."[6]

"I have loved you with an everlasting love; I have drawn you with loving-kindness."[7]

I also considered these words spoken for God through a prophet: "The Lord your God is with you, he is mighty to save. He will take great delight in you, he will quiet you with his love, he will rejoice over you with singing."[8]

I saw that God not only pined for us, but some writers also expressed a longing for God that sounded much like a man or woman separated from a lover:

"I myself will see him with my own eyes—I, and not another. How my heart yearns within me!"[9]

"As the deer pants for streams of water, so my soul pants for you, O God. My soul thirsts for God, for the living God. When can I go and meet with God?"[10]

"I long to dwell in your tent forever."[11]

"O God, you are my God, earnestly I seek you; my soul thirsts for you, my body longs for you, in a dry and weary land where there is no water."[12]

"How lovely is your dwelling place, O Lord Almighty! My soul yearns, even faints, for the courts of the Lord; my heart and my flesh cry out for the living God."[13]

Why Is Song of Songs in the Bible?

Why is Song of Songs in the canon of Scripture? There is no mention of God in its eight chapters. In fact, the open expression of sensuality makes some uncomfortable, wondering if such words should even be published in our Holy Book. I didn't even begin to quote the images of love that Solomon and the Shulamite woman said to each other. Some of their expressions sound a little strange to our modern, Western ears: breasts "like two fawns," neck "like an ivory tower," eyes that are "the pools of Heshbon" and a nose "like the tower of Lebanon looking toward Damascus." Most women wouldn't find those descriptions very flattering today. But for the Shulamite woman, this was the height of poetry. She was loved, and she knew it.

So, what is the purpose of glorifying physical love? Jewish and Christian scholars generally agree that Song of Solomon is part of Scripture for two reasons. First, it upholds a picture of marital love as it was intended. Here is a glimpse of what God desired when He joined man and wife in the Garden of Eden and told them to "be fruitful and multiply." For centuries, marriages have occurred for many reasons—for economic or political benefits, because the families got along, because the man needed an heir, because it was convenient and that's what young people did. But marriage primarily for reasons of love has become commonplace only in the last couple of centuries, and not in all parts of the world.

Is that what God really wanted marriage to be—an expression of passionate love? In the Song of Solomon, we glimpse the possibilities: Man and woman can thoroughly enjoy each other for life within the confines of marriage. Whether marriage emerges from a romance or is arranged, God's intention is that every married couple experience the fullness of romantic love for each other.

The song contains a note of caution. Twice the beloved warns: "Do not arouse or awaken love until it so desires." Rabbis for centuries forbade the reading of this book until a man turned thirty, afraid that these words might arouse inappropriate desires.

There is a second intention in this book, and both Jewish and Christian scholars have acknowledged it. The Song of Songs expresses God's love for His people. Before Christ, rabbis taught that this was God's love song for Abraham and his descendants. New Testament believers saw it as an expression of Christ's love for His church. Dennis F. Kinlaw writes in his commentary:

> Why is this seemingly erotic little book included in the sacred canon? The Bible does not see marriage as an inferior state, a concession to human weakness. Nor does it see the normal physical love within that relationship as impure.... The Song is a song in praise of love for love's sake and for love's sake alone. This relationship needs no justification beyond itself.
>
> The Song of Songs, however, is more than a declaration that human sexual love in itself is good. The use of the marriage metaphor to describe the relationship of God to his people is almost universal in Scripture.... Monogamous marriage is the norm for depicting the covenant relationship throughout Scripture, climaxing with the Marriage Supper of the Lamb.[14]

What does that say to me? It seemed that God was not only blessing our desire for romance and passion, but also that those feelings are a reflection of His desire for us. He loves us and wants us to revel together with Him in that love.

Lonely in Green Bay

Most people who get to know Jo and me want to hear our love story. It's part of who we are, and we gladly tell how we met, fell in love, and married.

Before marriage, my picture of happiness was contained in sports. From the time I was a boy growing up in New York City, my primary desire was to play major league baseball, preferably in Yankee Stadium, where my hero, Mickey Mantle, roamed center field.

The only problem was that I lacked the ability to hit a 90-mile-per-hour fastball or to curve a baseball consistently across the outside corner of home plate. So I did the next best thing: I wrote about sports. At least I could meet my heroes in the locker room and watch them perform from an ideal seat in the press box.

For several years after college, I edited a national sports magazine. Then I went to work with Pro Athletes Outreach, where I received my first book contract. It took me to the mecca of professional football, Green Bay, Wisconsin, to research a profile about a friend who played defensive tackle for the Packers. That Thanksgiving week I observed team practices, visited the Packers Hall of Fame, and had a pass for Lambeau Field that allowed me access anywhere in the stadium during the Packers' game against their arch rivals, the Chicago Bears. My 27th birthday also occurred that week, and I couldn't imagine a better way to celebrate it.

So, why wasn't I happy? Well, for one thing, the Packers and Bears happened to be playing on the second coldest day ever for an NFL game. Since I lived in Phoenix, Arizona, I didn't have the appropriate wardrobe. I layered every piece of clothing from my suitcase, but three pairs of socks were no barrier against the below-zero windchill as I roamed the sidelines.

Still, it was an exhilarating experience for a young writer working on his first book—except for my second problem. I had no one to share it with. As I thawed out in the motel that night, I was acutely aware of an intense loneliness. I had many friends. But I longed for someone to phone who was expecting my call, to whom I could relate all my experiences and hear on the other end that she was excited with me. I needed to know someone loved me and missed me and wanted to tell me all about what was happening in her life. Was there one person in this world who would care more about me than anyone else? Was there a single individual with whom I could share my dreams and my journey?

That night, in my motel room, I prayed this most urgent prayer: "God, would You give me a wife? Someone who will be my closest friend, with whom I can share my life?"

Five months later, while visiting a church in Paradise Valley, Arizona, I saw the answer to my prayer singing in the choir. After the service, a man sitting in the pew ahead of me invited me to the Sunday school class for singles. There were five people in the class, and one of them was Jo, the alto with the wonderful smile who sang in the choir. Afterward, the couple leading the class invited both of us to lunch. Since I had to leave town on business the next day, I asked Jo to pray for the trip. When I returned a week later, I tried to call her, but she was away from home every night. I finally reached her at six p.m. Saturday as her date for that evening was knocking on her door. After she laughed at my boldness in calling so late for a date, she agreed to have lunch with me the next day after church.

For me, the dating ritual had often felt like an act, with each person on his or her best behavior for as long as possible. Jo and I didn't play that game. During our first lunch, I told her about my spiritual journey and about my desire to find a friend with whom I could share my life. Amazingly, Jo shared that desire and was willing to explore the possibility of friendship with me. Jo's active dating life suddenly revolved around only one man. We were together every day for the next three weeks, and then I proposed to her in Encanto Park, and she accepted. Fifteen weeks later we were married!

My wife and I have warned our children and their friends not to try this approach. The speed at which our relationship developed is definitely not a model to copy. We moved quickly because we were in our late twenties and believed God had brought us together. We prayed about it and sought confirmation from family and friends, all of whom confirmed that Jo and I were a good match!

Ironically, while we were attracted to each other, neither of us felt a sizzling passion while we dated. The ardor was ignited after the wedding. There was an eagerness as we drove out of Phoenix toward Sedona for our honeymoon. And we weren't disappointed. That night together was so exciting that neither of us managed any sleep. Something was ignited in us when we came together, and that flame has never been extinguished.

The Expectations of Passion

What did I want when I met Jo? Was it happiness? Yes, but I think it was much more than that. Happiness is a by-product of having our expectations met. Those expectations seem fairly similar among the married couples I know. Jo and I want to know that we are the one and only person for each other. Sure, we have other friends, but ours is a far greater intimacy than we can know with anyone else. We also expect that we will always be there for each other—this relationship is for life. From the beginning, we have felt an excitement together, and we expect that this excitement will last and mature. There is also an expectation that we will sacrifice for each other, that I will give to Jo and she will give to me. No doubt we talked about these thoughts during our engagement, but when you're first married, you can't really explain your expectations. I'm sure I didn't understand them the way I do now, 30 years later.

I believe the intense longing I felt in Green Bay is common to most people. It's the way we were created. We desire intimacy, but there is no way we can know everyone and be known by them. We can only hope for the closest intimacy with one person. We may gain a taste of that intimacy, when growing up, through a few close friendships. Yet even there we never attain the total intimacy that is experienced only in marriage between one man and one woman.

Unfortunately, such closeness still is never achieved in many marriages. There is something dangerous and terribly risky about opening ourselves up to another individual. There is a latent fear that maybe my spouse won't like me if she knows what I'm really like. Do I dare reveal that deepest inner thought—what if my husband is horrified by it? And what if, as the years pass and I get to know my spouse, I find I don't really like this person as much as I thought I would?

As I reflect on this and talk with others, I sense that these feelings are part of the human condition, but usually they are not expressed or understood. For too many men, genuine intimacy is a terrifying thought. Often marriage is viewed as a goal to reach in life. Like a hunter stalking an elk, one picks out the prettiest girl he can find and sets out to win her affections. The objective is to get her to the altar, where she becomes committed to him. From that point on, she is his prize, played with in the bedroom, then dressed and shown for all to see and admire.

For too many women, their anticipation of intimacy is shattered with the realization that they are simply trophies. A woman wants to be admired for more than just her beauty, because she has much to give if her husband would only recognize it. Plus she has her own ambitions and dreams. But so often her husband acts as if his dreams are the only ones that matter, as if his wife should just naturally sacrifice everything for his career. When she does, there is peace in the home. When she balks, the husband frequently feels disoriented.

No wonder so many couples I've known are disappointed with marriage. There is so much more to it than the courtship. The wedding is supposed to be the beginning of a great journey, not the end.

Counterfeit Passion

There's another aspect to romance that must be addressed. I can't reflect on passion and romance without addressing the issue of fidelity. Our culture has emphatically rejected the idea that sexual intimacy is reserved only for the marriage bed. Movies and television shows have no problem depicting a boy and girl hopping into bed for any reason or no reason, whether they really know each other or not. Much of our popular music celebrates sexual pleasure. The message being shouted is "Do not deny your sexual feelings."

There is a countermessage. Abstinence campaigns like "True Love Waits" have been eagerly embraced by many teens. But often that message is drowned out by the predominance of sex in the media. The question is, does God truly intend for sex to be experienced only within marriage? The Scriptures are clear. Every reference to sexual activity outside of marriage is condemned. By contrast, marital intercourse is blessed by God and is the means whereby husband and wife become one flesh.

My intention, when I married, was to be completely faithful to Jo. My expectation, based on my commitment, was that I would have no desire to look at any other women. Reality has proved more difficult. A few years ago I was a long distance from home, teaching at a Christian writer's conference. During one of the afternoon sessions when writers can meet with editors, I was approached by an attractive woman, about 15 years younger than me, named Esther.* "This is the first chapter of a novel I've been working on for a couple of years," she explained. "I've never shown it to anyone before, but I'd like to know if you think it has potential."

Reviewing unpublished manuscripts at a writer's conference requires a balance of encouragement and honesty. Often the material is rough, and usually I am able, after a few minutes, to offer a writer several specific suggestions to guide her in her next draft.

So I didn't expect much from Esther's work. I read the first paragraph and was immediately gripped by both the story and the beautiful writing style. I turned to page two, then page three, and I couldn't stop reading.

"This is really quite remarkable," I said, barely looking up. After ten minutes of reading, I knew I had to stop and say something. "Do you have any more of the novel with you?" I asked.

Nervously, Esther pulled out a manuscript. "I have written 120 pages. This is all of it."

"Do you mind if I take it to my room and read it?"

For the first time, Esther smiled. She knew editors are busy and don't ask for more reading material except in rare circumstances. That night, I read the rest of the manuscript and was disappointed when the story stopped. I loved her characters, and I wanted to know what was going to happen to them.

Esther sat at my table for lunch the next day, and I told her I wanted to discuss the possible publication of her novel. However, with six other writers at the table, each also vying for my attention, we couldn't talk further. We met at the coffee shop later that afternoon. Several other editors were meeting with writers at tables throughout the restaurant.

"Esther," I said, "this is one of the best first novels I've seen. I do have a few suggestions, but I am very interested in seeing this book finished and published, hopefully by my company."

The young woman took out a notepad and pen and began to take notes. At one point, I stopped and looked at her. She was an attractive woman. I glanced at her left hand and noticed there was no ring on it. "How long have you been writing?" I asked.

"I majored in creative writing in college," she quietly explained. "I've been teaching high school English for the last five years, and I spend all my free time working on my writing. My parents have always said I have a gift, and I'm trying to be faithful to God to develop that gift."

For some reason I was touched by this young woman's sincerity. I have met many ambitious people who aspire to be successful authors. But this woman was different. She was serious about her craft. She had a spiritual depth that was unusual and very attractive. At that moment, a thought entered my mind: *If I weren't married, I'd want to date her.*

I saw a lot of Esther that week. She attended my classes, sat at my table for several meals, and found a way to speak to me on several occasions. Alone in my room at night, I thought about Esther and wondered what it would be like to have an evening of conversation with her away from the spotlight of a conference. It was exciting to interact with her. I had to admit, she was very attractive physically, but this was more. She was a godly woman, and she had talent.

A mental battle raged during my flight home because I couldn't shake the memory of this beautiful woman. I knew Jo was home with two small kids. I knew she'd greet me at the door with a smile and a kiss, and the aroma of a nice dinner would fill the house. But she would also be wearing jeans and a T-shirt, and she probably would have to hurry to change a diaper or wipe a runny nose. She couldn't compete with Esther's modest dresses, her youthful figure, and the exciting project we could be working on together. I felt guilty thinking about Esther, instead of my wife. *Lord*, I prayed, *please remove Esther from my thoughts.* One minute later, I was again thinking of her.

Most of us, even happily married couples, find ourselves occasionally battling such a temptation. It's not something we want to deal with; the temptation simply presents itself. Within a sex-saturated society, many people are fooled by these feelings, concluding, *I made a mistake and married the wrong person* or *Despite the fact that I'm married, this must be true love.* Others of us are snared by a more subtle lie. We think we're being faithful to our spouse as long as we don't actually become romantic or physical with someone else, forgetting that infidelity begins in the heart, in the emotions, in an inordinate desire for relationship with another human being. I can't avoid contact with another woman, but I can decide what I think about her and how I respond to her.

Over the years, I've had to awaken to the truth that the heart is much more deceitful than we give it credit for. Jesus said that adultery is a matter of the heart.[15] When I entertain improper thoughts or feelings, I am starting down the road that can lead eventually to physical adultery. The worst danger is to believe that "I could never do that" or that being really drawn to another woman is okay as long I don't get physically involved with her. Many well-intentioned Christian men have fallen for that lie and violated their marital vows because they failed to control their minds and hearts early on. I am much safer realizing that, apart from the grace of God, I am absolutely capable of being unfaithful to Jo.

Why didn't I pursue an affair with Esther? Certainly, there was fear of getting caught. I could lose my job, and my reputation in Christian publishing would be destroyed. There was also the fact that Jo would be horribly hurt if she ever found out, and she might divorce me. That would cause all sorts of financial and emotional hardships for both of us. Further, I wondered how I could look my kids in the eye and tell them to live holy and pure lives, knowing that message was a sham in my own life.

All those are valid reasons for remaining faithful to one's wedding vows. But I know too many men who have ignored those negative consequences, seemingly willing to pay the cost. That's why I find the picture of God's faithfulness to be more motivational. If He is faithful to His bride, then I can also be faithful to mine. Further, I'm now convinced that this is the road to genuine fulfillment.

Will Having It All Really Make You Happy?

Some people protest that if the Song of Songs is indeed Solomon's love story, it's a terribly flawed picture of marriage. There is a sad footnote to the romance of the last chapter. I wanted to end the story with these words: "And they lived happily ever after." But, of course, Solomon and Cindy didn't live happily ever after. They could have, and Cindy certainly thought they would at the time they were married. Then something went wrong. I don't know if it was a few months later, or a few years after their marriage, but the sad fact is that Solomon's eye wandered. By the end of his life, he had accumulated 700 wives and 300 concubines.

Commentators have wrestled with that fact. Some have argued that the Shulamite woman was Solomon's true love and that all his other wives were for political purposes, demonstrating his great wealth and power. Others prefer to make the Song a pure allegory with no historical significance. I choose to accept the song for what it appears to be, a passionate expression of Solomon's love for one woman, and I believe that God chose to elevate this song for the greater purpose of revealing His heart. We shouldn't confuse the writer with the message. God said David was a man after His own heart, yet David committed adultery and murder.

Solomon was given the chance to have all the material riches of life without limit. Near the end of his life, he reflected on all that he had and what it meant. Note the sadness and cynicism as he writes:

I thought in my heart, "Come now, I will test you with pleasure to find out what is good." But that also proved to be meaningless. "Laughter," I said, "is foolish. And what does pleasure accomplish?"...

I acquired men and women singers, and a harem as well—the delights of the heart of man....

I denied myself nothing my eyes desired; I refused my heart no pleasure.

My heart took delight in all my work, and this was the reward for all my labor.

Yet when I surveyed all that my hands had done and what I had toiled to achieve, everything was meaningless, a chasing after the wind; nothing was gained under the sun.[16]

This is an important message for today's sex-saturated culture. Perhaps our obsession with fulfilling the lust of the flesh outside the confines of marriage doesn't lead to the happiness we desire. Solomon found true love and expressed it in his song. But rather than focusing on that love of his youth, he let his eye wander. God allowed him to have everything he wanted, including unlimited sexual pleasure. But that pleasure was not fulfilling. He was far happier when he was in a monogamous marriage.

Meaning in the Passion

The story of Solomon clearly shows that the message of our culture is a lie. I am far more motivated by God's picture of passion. This New Testament passage says it most clearly:

The body is not meant for sexual immorality, but for the Lord, and the Lord for the body.... Do you not know that your bodies are members of Christ himself? Shall I then take the members of Christ and unite them with a prostitute? Never! Do you not know that he who unites himself with a prostitute is one with her in body? For it is said, "The two will become one flesh." But he who unites himself with the Lord is one with him in spirit.[17]

Here is the real meaning of fidelity. Sexual intimacy within marriage is a picture of how God desires to unite with us in spirit. That is why Jo and I reject the culture's message and instead choose to lift our minds to this marvelous picture. To settle for anything less is to purchase a counterfeit.

So now we know the ideal. God wants us to enjoy a passionate marriage because that reflects His heart for us. But of course, God's marriage hasn't been "happily ever after." In fact, you might say His relationship with His beloved is more combative than romantic. That leads us to explore another aspect of God's love.

10

God Fights with His Beloved

When I explore God's marriage, one surprising element jumps out—His jealousy. God gets angry when His beloved drifts away from Him, and He challenges her to return. This next vignette concentrates on the prophets, who were the mouthpieces God used to express His anger and frustration over the actions of His beloved. Again, I want to explore this from the angels' point of view.[1]

Abdiel and Zephon stared at the scene with the morbid fascination of witnesses observing a horrible tragedy. They didn't want to look, but they couldn't help watching. God's beloved was behaving in a most bizarre manner, at least from the perspective of these angels. The people streamed out of the holy city of Jerusalem and wound their way up the nearby mountain, being joined by others from surrounding villages.

At the top of this mountain stood the object of affection for these people—a tall wooden statue of a naked woman, pregnant

100   your
m a r r i a g e
masterpiece

and holding out full breasts in invitation to her supplicants. As the crowd gathered around the idol, Abdiel shook his head in disbelief. "Why do they do this?" he asked his friend, barely able to contain his emotions.

"It's springtime," Zephon answered. "The people think that by honoring this fertility goddess, they will assure that their fields receive the necessary rain and that their crops will have a plentiful yield."

"Which explains the statue's pregnant belly and full breasts. But this is a goddess of the Canaanites, isn't it?"

"Yes, the same people God commanded to be destroyed. God's chosen people should have nothing to do with these detestable, so-called gods."

"Don't they realize that this statue can do nothing for them?"

The two angels watched as the priests and priestesses of Ash-toreth led the crowd in chants and prayers, petitioning the goddess for rain and healthy crops. Gradually, emotions grew among the crowd as the intensity of worship increased. Then the high priest and priestess removed their clothes and embraced each other. The angels turned away. "I can't stand this!" said Zephon. "It will degen-erate from here, and soon everyone will be involved in the orgy."

"As though their sexual passions will make a difference to a stupid statue," muttered Abdiel.

"Much less result in good crops," said Zephon.

"Why does He allow it? Why doesn't He do something!"

Abdiel's outburst was interrupted by a shout from another angel.

"Over here! Come look!"

Abdiel and Zephon hurried over to where a crowd of angels were observing their Master in intense discussion with a teenage boy. "Before you were born, I knew you," said the Lord. "Before you were born, I set you apart; I appointed you as a prophet to the nations."

The youngster shuddered at these words and bowed so low that his head touched the floor. Weakly, the boy spoke, "Oh, Sovereign Lord, I am only a child. I do not know how to speak."

"Do not say, 'I am only a child,'" God replied. "You must go to everyone I send you to and say whatever I command you." The boy was now shaking in terror at the presence of his God and at the words he was hearing. "Do not be afraid of them, for I am with you and will rescue you."

Then the angels saw an amazing sight: God reached out His hand and touched the boy's mouth. "I have put My words in your mouth," He said.

The angels couldn't believe God was choosing this feeble teenager to be His mouthpiece. "Wouldn't it make more sense to send Michael or Gabriel?" said Abdiel.

"For some reason, our Lord doesn't want to use supernatural forces with these people. He prefers to use ordinary men."

"But this one is so young and so weak. You would think He'd at least choose a real man, someone with an imposing physique who could command the respect of his hearers."

"Hush! Let's hear what our Master is saying to the young man."

"Get yourself ready!" the Lord's words rang out. The youngster scrambled to his feet as instructions continued. "Stand up and say to them whatever I command you. Do not be terrified by them, or I will terrify you before them." Abdiel couldn't suppress a chuckle, thinking how terrified the boy was already. "Today I have made you a fortified city, an iron pillar, and a bronze wall to stand against the whole land—against the kings of Judah, its officials, its priests, and the people of the land. They will fight against you but will not overcome you, for I am with you and will rescue you."

"Wow!" Abdiel exclaimed. "He just told this feeble kid that he's impregnable."

The angels heard another commotion. "Hey! Come see this!"

102   your
m a r r i a g e
masterpiece

an angel shouted. Abdiel and Zephon hurried over to the place and saw their Master talking to another person, this one a grown man of about 30. The man was dressed in rags, as were the other exiles of Israel who were now living in the foreign land of Babylon. This man looked just as terrified as the teenager to whom God had spoken. He had just seen a glimpse of God's glory, and he fell prone on his face, unable to look at the sight before him. But as with the boy, God reached down and touched this man.

"Son of man, stand up on your feet and I will speak to you," He said as he grabbed the man's arm and pulled him up. "Son of man, I am sending you to the Israelites, to a rebellious nation that has rebelled against Me; they and their fathers have been in revolt against Me to this very day."

"That's right!" Abdiel yelled.

Zephon calmed his friend with a hand to his shoulder, and they overheard God's instructions to the man dressed in rags.

"Do not be afraid, though briers and thorns are all around you and you live among scorpions. Do not be afraid of what they say or be terrified by them, though they are a rebellious house. You must speak My words to them, whether they listen or fail to listen." And with many more words, God prepared this man for his unique mission.

The angels bounced back and forth between the youngster and the older man, and they also listened to other prophets speak God's words against the people. The teenager boldly spoke God's message to a crowd inside Jerusalem. "I remember the devotion of your youth, how as a bride you loved Me and followed Me through the desert, through a land not sown." The boy started softly, tenderly, but soon his voice had risen. "Does a maiden forget her jewelry, a bride her wedding ornaments? Yet My people have forgotten Me days without number," yelled the young man. "How skilled you are at pursuing love! Even the worst of women can learn from your ways."

The angels were astonished at his boldness, especially because the crowd was laughing at him and jeering at him.

"What do you know about love?" yelled one man in the audience. The crowd laughed, encouraging another heckler to yell, "You're too young to have a wife! Who are you to tell us about marriage?"

For the citizens of Jerusalem, this seemed like great entertainment.

"Listen to him!" Abdiel yelled, though he knew the crowd couldn't hear his exhortation.

The teenager seemed stunned for a moment but then continued on with God's message. "If a man divorces his wife and she leaves him and marries another man, should he return to her again? Would not the land be completely defiled? But you have lived as a prostitute with many lovers—would you now return to Me?" The boy pointed to the hills around Jerusalem. Abdiel particularly noted his emphasis on the spot where the people had gone and worshiped Ashtoreth, the fertility goddess. "Look up to the barren heights and see. Is there any place where you have not been ravished? By the roadside you sat waiting for lovers, sat like a nomad in the desert. You have defiled the land with your prostitution and wickedness. Therefore, the showers have been withheld and no spring rains have fallen. Yet you have the brazen look of a prostitute; you refuse to blush with shame."

Zephon shook his head and turned away. "How can they listen to those words and not be filled with shame?"

"They seem oblivious," said Abdiel. "He insults them and they laugh. He pleads with them and they shrug their shoulders. If they would only listen! You can tell how much our Lord hurts, how much He desires them."

The young prophet was in tears now as he said, "'Return, faithless people,' declares the Lord, 'for I am merciful. I will not be angry forever. Only acknowledge your guilt—you have rebelled against the Lord your God, you have scattered your favors to foreign gods under every spreading tree, and have not obeyed Me,' declares the Lord. 'Return, faithless people,' declares the Lord, 'for I am your husband.'"

"They can't possibly resist that!" said Zephon. "Which of us wouldn't respond instantly to such longing?"

"We wouldn't have left Him in the first place," said Abdiel.

"But the Creator doesn't desire us in the same way. He wants those weak, fickle creatures." Zephon stopped himself. "No, I mustn't say that. If that is His longing, then we must try to understand why He is so patient with them."

"I'd have simply wiped them out," said Abdiel. "He is doing everything imaginable to win them back. Look at the 10 tribes He has had rounded up and taken as slaves to Babylon."

With that, they switched their attentions to the other prophet, who at this moment was getting instructions from the Lord Himself. The angels were shocked to hear their Master speak so forcefully. "Son of man, confront Jerusalem with her detestable practices." It was a long speech that the prophet would repeat later to all who would listen. The angels were enraptured as their Lord spoke: "On the day you were born, your cord was not cut, nor were you washed with water to make you clean, nor were you rubbed with salt or wrapped in cloths. No one looked on you with pity or had compassion enough to do any of these things for you. Rather, you were thrown into the open field, for on the day you were born, you were despised.

"Then I passed by and saw you kicking about in your blood, and as you lay there in your blood I said to you, 'Live!' I made you grow like a plant of the field. You grew up and developed and became the most beautiful of jewels. Your breasts were formed and your hair grew; you who were naked and bare."

The Lord paused in His recitation, apparently filled with emotion. The angels marveled at their Master's tenderness as He recalled a past memory. He continued speaking to the prophet: "Later, I passed by, and when I looked at you and saw that you were old enough for love, I declared my intention and desire to make you My wife."[2] The Lord was nearly in tears as He softly remembered that moment. "I gave you My solemn oath and entered into a covenant with you. You became Mine."

The Lord paced as He spoke, the words spilling out rapidly as He began recalling all the things He'd done for His bride. "I clothed you with an embroidered dress and put leather sandals on you. I dressed you in fine linen and covered you with costly garments. I adorned you with jewelry: I put bracelets on your arms and a necklace around your neck, and I put earrings on your ears and a beautiful crown on your head. So you were adorned with gold and silver; your clothes were of fine linen and costly fabric and embroidered cloth. Your food was fine flour, honey, and olive oil. You became very beautiful and rose to be a queen. Your fame spread on account of your beauty, because the splendor I had given you made your beauty perfect."

The angels could almost hear the protest of God's intended audience. "Nonsense!" the wife might interrupt. "You had nothing to do with my beauty. Sure, You gave me some things, but my beauty is mine, and I'll use it as I wish. Frankly, others seem to appreciate it more than You do."

The Creator anticipated that protest, and His voice rose as He said, "But you trusted in your beauty and used your fame to become a prostitute. You lavished your favors on anyone who passed by, and your beauty became his. You took some of your garments to make gaudy high places where you carried on your prostitution. Such things should not happen, nor should they ever occur."

106   your
m a r r i a g e
masterpiece

The Lord's voice continued to rise until now He was practically shouting as He said, "You took your sons and daughters, whom you bore to Me, and sacrificed them as food to the idols." The angels held their breath as their Master yelled, "Was your prostitution not enough? You slaughtered My children and sacrificed them to the idols. In all your detestable practices and your prostitution you did not remember the days of your youth, when you were naked and bare, kicking about in your blood."

The angels shuddered. Recalling one of the gods the Israelites often worshiped, Zephon whispered to his friend, "You know, it just dawned on me. Do you know what the name *Baal* means?"

Abdiel looked at Zephon and answered, "I think it means 'owner' or 'master.'"

"Yes, it can mean that. Or it can mean—" He hesitated to say the word. "It can mean 'husband.' I just realized the full significance of this explosion of anger. These people aren't just turning their allegiance away from our Lord and Master. They are allowing another god, a cheap imitation, a total fraud, to assume the role of husband to the one He, our Lord, loves."

"That's why He's so passionate. Listen!"

The Lord was wagging His finger at the prophet as He continued His diatribe: "I stretched out My hand against you and reduced your territory; I gave you over to the greed of your enemies, who were shocked by your lewd conduct. And even after that, you still were not satisfied. How weak-willed you are when you do all these things, acting like a brazen prostitute!

"You adulterous wife! You prefer strangers to your own husband! Every prostitute receives a fee, but you give gifts to all your lovers, bribing them to come to you from everywhere for your illicit favors. So in your prostitution you are the opposite of others; no one runs after you for your favors. You are the very opposite, for you give payment and none is given to you."

The angels could almost hear the wife sneering words like "So, what are you going to do about it?"

God anticipated that, too: "I am going to gather all your lovers. I will gather them against you from all around and will strip you in front of them and they will see all your nakedness. I will sentence you to the punishment of women who commit adultery and who shed blood; I will bring upon you the blood vengeance of My wrath and jealous anger. Then I will hand you over to your lovers. They will bring a mob against you, who will stone you and hack you to pieces with their swords. They will burn down your houses and inflict punishment on you in the sight of many women. I will put a stop to your prostitution, and you will no longer pay your lovers."

Zephon rubbed his chin and observed, "You know, I've never seen Him this angry."

Abdiel agreed. "Even when He tossed Lucifer and the other rebels out of heaven, He wasn't upset like this. I don't understand why this is such a huge deal to Him. Lucifer was His favorite in heaven, but God seems to care far more about these people."

"I think the difference is love," said Zephon. "He didn't love Lucifer in the same way He loves Israel."

The Lord was speaking softly, tenderly again. "I will deal with you as you deserve, because you have despised My oath by breaking the covenant. Yet I will remember the covenant I made with you in the days of your youth, and I will establish an everlasting covenant with you. Then you will remember your ways and be ashamed. When I make atonement for all you have done, you will remember and be ashamed and never again open your mouth because of your humiliation."

"I don't understand this thing you call love," said Abdiel, shaking his head. "I can see what you are talking about. But it doesn't make sense."

"No, it doesn't," agreed Zephon. "Why should one He cares so deeply for be allowed to abuse Him and spit at His devotion? Wouldn't any one of us gladly respond to an offer of affection from our Creator? Yes, we would bow down and worship Him even more if He showed us such care. But He gives His affection to these creatures, and they despise Him."

"Still, He won't give up," Abdiel observed. "I wonder, is there anything He can do to win back their love?"

"That is a profound question. I have no idea what more He can do to demonstrate His love. But obviously, He's not about to quit. So there probably is something more He plans to do. He says He will make atonement for His beloved. We will have to see what that means."

11

The Fighting Marriage

I vaguely remember how, when I was three years old, my family moved from Connecticut to Queens in New York City. The night our family of four moved into a one-bedroom apartment, the couple in the apartment above us were having a heated argument. Sleep was impossible until finally the husband left about three A.M., slamming the door behind him with a viciousness that shook the building. As far as we know, the man never returned.

Many years later, Jo and I were living in a Portland suburb with our two small boys and newborn baby girl. One hot summer night, we pitched a tent in the backyard for the boys. As Joshua and Jonathan drifted off to sleep, the couple behind our house began to fight. Since none of us in the neighborhood had air-conditioning, and it was too hot to close the windows, everyone heard the argument, punctuated by louder and increasing uses of the "f" word. Amazingly, our sons slept through the battle. Finally, we heard a loud slap of hand hitting flesh, followed by a woman's wail. The argument was over.

It was hard to imagine that those two people ever cared for one another, let alone stood in front of an altar pledging to love and cherish each other until death.

Most of us know we shouldn't eavesdrop on a marital spat, but when we inadvertently hear one, it's almost impossible to ignore. Consumed with uncontrollable passion and rage, the combatants aren't thinking about who might overhear. These are not civil discussions characterized by cold indifference. When lovers quarrel, sparks fly!

God's Heart Is Broken

There are many people today who say they can't accept the God of the Old Testament because He is so judgmental. His wrath scares people, and with good reason. Sometimes it feels as though God's anger is totally out of control. Naturally, many people prefer to worship only a God of love. They view God as a caring deity who would never hurt anyone. On the other hand, some of these same people get angry with a loving God whom they perceive to be indifferent to their suffering. They would like to see God execute justice on those who hurt them.

So which God is He—a God of love or a God of anger? I found it difficult to reconcile the two until I began to see God as a jilted lover. Because He loves so passionately, He gets angry when His love is spurned. In that context, God's wild emotions make sense.

John Eldredge has described reading the prophets as the equivalent of overhearing a man and wife fighting in the next room.[1] That's a pretty accurate assessment. When we think about how we've been hurt in our relationships, we recognize many of the same emotions in God's indictment of Israel. I've concluded that God loves His people with great passion, and the evidence of that passion is most apparent when He angrily confronts idolatry. It's not unlike a man catching his wife in bed with another lover.

The Bible records many heated encounters between God and Israel. The observations by the two angels in chapter ten were inspired by the prophets Jeremiah and Ezekiel. We could have looked in Isaiah or Hosea and discovered similar reproaches. Most of the marital fights are rather one-sided: God does most of the yelling. After listening to Him for a while, I have to wonder what person in his right mind would put up with such an unfaithful spouse.

God considered the nation of Israel His wife. He'd made a covenant, an irrevocable commitment to her, and He was hurt—just as any one of us would be—when His wife committed adultery. But the worst feeling came when His beloved not only was seduced by other lovers (other gods) but actively chose to pursue those worthless imitations. How could she worship wood and stone replicas of creation when she was married to the One who created all things? To God, this was inconceivable!

Did God consider divorce? He certainly had grounds. Listen to Him speaking through Jeremiah: "I gave faithless Israel her certificate of divorce and sent her away because of all her adulteries."[2] But if He has divorced Israel, He goes right on pleading for her love, calling her back to Himself. So did He really divorce her, or did He use hyperbole to make His point? My understanding of the Mosaic Law is that divorce was allowed. Jesus Himself acknowledged that but added the caveat that divorce was never God's intention. It was put in the law only because the hearts of people were hard.[3]

When I set aside my assumptions about the God I've worshiped in nice churches for 50-plus years, I'd say He sounds a lot like a frantic lover who will say and do almost anything to save His marriage. Well, perhaps that is the case. Maybe my modern image of God is too tame. When I read the prophets, I hear God's heart breaking. But He wasn't simply a complaining God. He took action and disciplined Israel with tough love. There had to be a separation for a while so that issues could be dealt with and healing might occur. This relationship was far too important to let things slide. God wanted His love back, and He was determined to do whatever was necessary to accomplish that.

To Fight or Not to Fight

Some people seem to enjoy a good argument. I am not one of them. In our marriage, my tendency is to avoid confrontation. However, if I'm cornered and have to fight, then I fight to win. I recall one situation where Jo was angry because I had carelessly missed a bag of groceries when I unloaded the car after a trip to the supermarket. Jo discovered the spoiled meat the next day and called me at the office. When I arrived home, she egged me on. How could I miss something so obvious? Didn't I know we were on a tight budget and couldn't afford to be careless? But I wouldn't respond. I was plenty angry myself, but rather than argue, I went to the garage, grabbed the lawn mower, and worked out my anger on the back lawn.

Because of my personality, Jo and I rarely engage in shouting matches. But we have had some intense disagreements. Early in our marriage, I began to notice that there were certain periods when I could do little right in my wife's eyes. She would snip at me and blame me for things that at other times didn't bother her at all. One day it dawned on me that I could predict exactly when those outbursts would occur. We talked about it, and Jo told me later that she realized she was projecting negative emotions on me during her menstrual cycle, and she recognized that wasn't fair. She decided she had a choice—to hurt our relationship by lashing out, or to recognize that she was hormonal and bite her tongue. Life became more peaceful after that.

However, there have been occasions when Jo has rightfully challenged me. One of the most memorable was after the birth of our third child, Anna. For six years, we had lived in Salem, Oregon, where I was a full-time freelance writer and wrote 17 books for various clients. Jo was an integral part of this business. She answered the phone, tracked our finances, critiqued my writing, and provided a listening ear when I needed to talk through a project. We were truly partners. My office was a converted garage, and I could come into the house anytime to get a cup of coffee, kiss my wife, and hug my two sons.

That changed when I took an editorial position with a publishing company in Portland. Jo was pregnant with Anna when we sold our house and moved to Gresham, a suburb east of Portland. There she found herself without her friends, with no church home, in a new neighborhood, caring for a newborn baby and two active sons. But perhaps hardest of all, she was no longer a partner with her husband. I got up in the morning and drove to work, where I interacted all day with people. When I returned home, Jo was hungry to hear all about it, but I was talked out.

When I did talk about work, much of it revolved around what I was learning from the president of the company. Jo began to resent this man, who had become a mentor in my life. While I loved my new job, Jo felt as though she had lost her husband. When Jo would bring up her frustrations, I simply didn't understand why she was feeling these emotions. Only in retrospect did it dawn on me that these were the toughest years for Jo, and I didn't give her the support she needed. My priorities were wrong, because I had segmented my life from hers. We were no longer partners together in a journey. This wasn't the way our marriage should be, and I needed to listen to my wife and make some corrections.

The Marriage Fight

Just as a healthy couple should feel free to vent to each other, so God invites His beloved to come to Him and speak honestly. In the

Psalms, the beloved's expressions of grief and anger are freely vented without any fear of rebuke: "My God, my God, why have you forsaken me? Why are you so far from saving me?"[4] "O LORD, the God who avenges, O God who avenges, shine forth.... pay back to the proud what they deserve. How long will the wicked, O Lord, how long will the wicked be jubilant?"[5]

But God is definitely not a phlegmatic observer. He lets His beloved know how He feels.

God's battles with His beloved weren't nearly as tame as my fights with Jo. Sometimes He sounded like a jealous husband; other times, like an ignored lover. "The wild animals honor me," He says through Isaiah, "...because I provide water in the desert...to give drink to my people, my chosen, the people I formed for myself that they may proclaim my praise. Yet you have not called upon me, O Jacob. You have not wearied yourselves for me, O Israel."[6] To me, He sounds a little like a weary husband who works very hard and whose wife doesn't appreciate it.

Why do couples fight? My battles with Jo all revolve around expectations. My wife expects me to tell her I love her, give her some time each day to talk, be mentally engaged when we're at the dinner table, pay attention to our children, and provide active leadership as their father. When I fail in one of these areas, she will let me know—gently at first, but more forcefully if I fail to listen. The bigger the expectation, the greater the protest when it isn't met.

God also has expectations of His beloved. When God married the nation of Israel, He did so with His eyes wide open. He loved her beyond measure. But He also knew that she was imperfect. He was ready to forgive her sins, and He offered that forgiveness many times when she turned back to Him. He also expected her to do what she should and could do, and He got very angry when she didn't even provide Him with the basic courtesies any husband can expect.

I can't help but be impressed with how hard God fights for His marriage. If there is one alarming trend now in the culture, it's the number of "amicable" divorces. I hear of couples simply drifting apart. They say they don't love each other anymore; there is no passion, so they go their separate ways. There is no battle at all for the marriage. Is it because couples don't expect much from their marriages? We fight passionately for those things we care most about.

How to Have a Good Fight

It occurs to me as I review passage after passage of God's challenges to His beloved that maybe His anger shows us when and how to fight within a marriage. First, God's complaints are based on the covenant. It's interesting that He held the people of Israel to a much higher standard than other nations. He had given Himself to them as their God, and they had agreed to be faithful to Him alone. Heaven forbid that God should ever go back on His word, but if He had, the people could have rightly called Him to account.

In fact, there is one situation where that happened. God was angry with His people after they built a golden calf to worship while God was giving Moses the law on Mount Sinai. God told Moses to get out of His way so He could destroy them. "Then," He said, "I will make you into a great nation."[7] You'd think this was a golden opportunity for Moses. But Moses didn't see it that way. He appealed to God: "Remember your servants Abraham, Isaac and Israel to whom you swore by your own self: 'I will make your descendants as numerous as the stars in the sky.'"[8]

Moses had every right to challenge God based on the covenant. Because of that appeal, God relented and did not follow through on His threat. God, likewise, had every right to challenge Israel's unfaithfulness, and He did so based on the fact that they were married.

A friend of mine, Pete*, struggled with an addiction to pornography. When his wife discovered the problem, she confronted him.

At first he dismissed her accusations. "This is no big deal," he said. "Why are you upset?"

"Because we're married," she calmly explained through her tears. "I love you. I'm here for you. You don't need these other women."

"But they're just pictures!" he protested. "They mean nothing."

"Then give them up," his wife pleaded.

But my friend didn't. Pete simply did a better job of hiding the evidence. Once I became aware of his struggle, I would occasionally ask him how he was doing, and every time he would say he had the problem under control. But gradually I saw him less and less frequently. Pete's wife was right to be concerned, for over time her husband's problems increased. He started calling 900 numbers and visiting strip clubs. When she discovered the evidence on credit card bills, they had a far greater confrontation. Despite her evidence, Pete refused to admit he had a problem and get help. We'll come back to Pete in a minute.

My second observation is God's astonishing patience. I find this hard to understand, for in our culture we have a quick-fix mentality. We don't allow much time for a person to change. But God spent hundreds of years fighting for this marriage. He continually reached out to His beloved. "Come back to me!" He'd plead. Sometimes she did. Occasionally hard times were required—famine or conquest by enemies—to bring her to her senses. Then she'd cry out for mercy and God always responded. My human attitude would have been to let her stew a little longer in her misery—it served her right.

It's sad how many couples aren't willing to persevere. But in a self-centered society, if I'm not happy, I don't have much patience. I want my happiness now!

I once knew a couple who had been married for six years. They'd met and married quickly, before they really knew each other. It soon became evident that he was abusive. Emotionally,

Jack* had to dominate Nancy*, and he used Christianity as his primary control mechanism. She was expected to follow his every order without debate. Nancy was a sweet girl and tried to please Jack, but he was never satisfied. She begged him to go to counseling, and they did—for two sessions, after which Jack announced that he was fine. She could keep going if she wanted, but Jack didn't need any more help.

Finally, Nancy had had enough. She convinced herself that she couldn't endure the abuse any longer. There was no evidence of unfaithfulness by Jack, though he was admittedly not nice to live with. Friends at church tried to encourage Nancy to try other approaches to save the marriage. But Nancy was fed up and wouldn't consider other options. She took her daughter, left Jack, and filed for divorce. She was a hard worker and went to school while working a job to support her daughter. The daughter struggled in school and suffered emotionally. Jack remarried and divorced again three years later.

There is a sad footnote to this story. After Jack's second divorce, he had a nervous breakdown and was placed in a mental institution. Doctors there diagnosed a mental illness that had plagued Jack for most of his life. Fortunately, the illness was treatable and he is doing quite well now. I couldn't help but wonder what might have happened if Nancy had persevered a little longer, done a little more research, and obtained a little more help. Perhaps they could have discovered Jack's problem and eventually had a happy marriage, saving themselves, their daughter, and their extended families a lot of relational pain. We'll never know.

Caring Enough to Confront

Finally, I note that God isn't passive about the problems of His marriage. God didn't just endure Israel's unfaithfulness. He didn't simply vent His emotions; He also took constructive action. For Israel, that meant tough love. That meant separation for a time so she could work out her problems.

There is nothing spiritual about being a doormat. A spouse should not tolerate or endure unending abuse, whether physical or emotional. When a husband abuses his wife and demands she submit and accept that abuse, it's wrong. This is not the love that was promised in the covenant. Nancy thought her choices were either to endure Jack's abuse or to leave him. She never considered tough love. Nancy could and should have confronted Jack, and when he didn't respond, she had every right to take whatever steps were necessary, perhaps including a temporary separation, to ensure that he got the help he needed.

Dr. James Dobson powerfully addresses this in his book *Love Must Be Tough*. Much of the book deals with the problem of infidelity in marriage. After looking at several cases in which adultery was allowed for an extended period by a spouse, he writes, "No one labeled the behavior for what it was: selfishness and sin! Therein lies a fundamental problem. These loving, gracious people inadvertently shielded their wayward spouses from the consequences of infidelity. If there is *anything* that an adulterer does not need, it is a guilt-ridden mate who understands his indiscretion and assumes the blame for it. Such a person needs to be called to *accountability*, not excused by rationalization!"[9]

Pete's wife exercised tough love when he refused to deal honestly with his sexual addiction. After she confronted him with the evidence, she insisted he move out. "I do not want a divorce," she said. "I love you, Pete. But what you are doing is wrong. It is hurting me, and it is hurting our children. We cannot continue to live this way. When you are willing to get help and become the man God created you to be, then I will welcome you back."

These words and actions were a wake-up call for Pete. He did seek help, and though there were several setbacks, the couple was reconciled a year later. Without his wife's tough love, I seriously doubt whether Pete would have changed.

It occurs to me that too many couples let important issues slide until they become major problems. Jo and I have decided to keep a very tight hedge of protection around our marriage. That means dealing with any concern quickly before it becomes a problem. A few years ago, Jo observed me interacting with a woman in our neighborhood. We shared an interest in writing, so we naturally talked about writing whenever our paths crossed. Jo and I occasionally socialized with this woman and her husband, and we saw them at neighborhood gatherings. One day, while Jo and I were walking, she said, "Al, I need to say something, and I've prayed about it and thought about how to bring this up. I don't want you to get angry. Please just hear me out." She then proceeded to tell me how this woman was attracted to me, and how I encouraged it by sitting next to her instead of Jo on a number of occasions. "I want you to be aware of this. It hurts me when you do this." She referred to a recent neighborhood gathering where there were some new faces. "They probably thought this woman was your wife, rather than me."

I was not offended by Jo's protest. For one thing, I knew I felt no attraction to this woman, but if I had, that would have been all the more reason to heed my wife's words. I also knew Jo is generally a secure woman. She saw something about this woman's feelings that I didn't. If she detected a threat to our marriage, I would do whatever it took to make us both feel safe. Jo had every right to appeal to me, based on our covenant. And I can do the same with her. Our marriage must be protected at all costs![10]

My conclusion from Scripture is that if God feels His marriage is worth fighting for, mine is worth fighting for too. God wasn't silent about how He felt when His marriage was threatened. He pleaded, cajoled, shouted, argued, insulted, and expressed in many ways His deep and undying love. The point is clear—He wanted His wife back, and He'd say whatever was necessary to draw her to Himself.

Today, with our busy lives, I have to wonder if we are willing to invest the emotional energy to fight for our marriages. In so many homes, it seems that the default button is silence. Someone is hurt but doesn't confront the problem. How many marriages have failed because a spouse wasn't willing to speak up and fight for their relationship?

Which raises another question. It's one thing to argue in a marriage when both partners care about the relationship. But suppose one person is apathetic or physically unable to give much to the marriage. Or worse, what if the spouse is actively rebelling against God and the partner? How far does a person go when she feels she is getting nothing back from her husband?

We've seen that God is willing to fight for His marriage. This next vignette demonstrates how far God is willing to go to *prove* His love and make His marriage last.

12

The Great Scandal

This biblical vignette is an important picture of God's determination to save His marriage. By extension, I believe it demonstrates the high value He places on us and our marriages. To help us better understand this facet of God's love for His bride, I have chosen to set the story in a contemporary context.

Joseph had a problem. For two years he'd been a youth pastor at a church of about 300 members. But he had no wife. It's not that he wanted to be single, and certainly his congregation expected him to marry. Church potlucks were the roughest times for the young man. Some well-intentioned lady would inevitably corner him and say something like "I know just the girl for you...." Joe always listened respectfully and had actually dated some of the girls. But every time he began to get the least bit serious, he'd remember Georgine. No one would ever have his heart except her.

Georgine had been Joe's boyhood love. She was the beauty with the honey-brown hair who lived down the street. As kids, they'd played together on the nearby playground. Somehow, as they grew

122   your
m a r r i a g e
masterpiece

older, Joe just knew they would get married. But Georgine had a horrible secret in her family, and as she entered into her teen years, the horror she experienced from her stepfather and uncle was too much to bear. Shortly after her 14th birthday, she ran away from home.

At first, Joe found it impossible to believe the stories, that she was living on the street in a distant city and making a living with her body. His mind rebelled at the thought of his beautiful friend being mistreated this way. Every time he thought of her, he'd pray, *Lord, protect her. Bring her help and draw her to Yourself.*

Then one Saturday evening, after another potluck encounter with a persistent matchmaking grandmother, Joe cried out in prayer, *Lord, what good is it for me to be in ministry if I have to go it alone? I want a partner to share this work with me.* And in that moment, he sensed God's answer. It wasn't audible, but it was very clear.

Joe responded immediately. He grabbed a suitcase and began packing. He jumped in his car and started driving toward that city several hundred miles away. He had no idea how he was going to find her, but he would search until he did, knowing God would guide him. He wasn't sure where to begin. Where does one find the red-light district when one has never sought out ladies of the night? Joe had a map, and he systematically began driving up and down the streets of downtown.

He almost missed her. It was nearly midnight. Joe had stopped at a signal, and a woman leaned against his car, talking through the open window. "Hey, handsome, want some real fun?" There, a block ahead of him, leaning against a lamppost—he instantly recognized her. As soon as the light changed, he drove slowly up the street. She didn't see him, but it was definitely Georgine. He drove another block, parked on a side street, and walked back. He observed her from behind. She'd dyed her hair blond, and it was teased to three times its normal size. She was wearing a tight red blouse and a miniskirt that barely covered her buttocks. But Joe stared at the profile of her face, already showing wrinkles from years of the hard life.

She noticed him out of the corner of her eye. "Like what you see?" she practically sneered. "Then make an offer, kid."

Joe gulped. "Georgine. Is that you?"

The name stunned the prostitute and she stared at him. "Joe? Well, I'll be... What are you doing here?"

"You probably won't believe this, but I was looking for you."

They drove home in the early dawn. Georgine cried most of the way. "You don't want me," she said as they entered his hometown.

"But I do," Joe protested.

"No, you don't know who I am. You don't know what I've done."

"Maybe so. But I love you. And, I remind you, you did come with me."

"Well, don't get your hopes up. I'm not sure yet whether I'll stay or not."

Joe's first step was to find a place for Georgine to live. He called a sweet older woman from his church who had an extra room, and she agreed to help out. The next morning, Joe picked Georgine up and drove her to church. That's when the excitement really started. Georgine sat in the front row of church, crossed her legs, and instantly had the embarrassed attention of the choir and ministers sitting on the stage. After service, the members shot Joe and Georgine nervous glances, but only a few teenagers talked to them.

After the coffee hour, Joe introduced Georgine to the senior pastor. "This is a very special friend," he said. "She's had a tough time, but I believe God is calling her to Himself."

124   your
m a r r i a g e
masterpiece

The pastor was gracious and extended his hand to her. "You are welcome here."

And indeed she was. When the women of the church realized that Georgine was an old friend of Joe's and in need, they pitched in to help. By the following Sunday, she was in church dressed in a modest floral-print dress. The women seemed pleased to have this ministry opportunity.

Then Joe made an announcement. He and Georgine were getting married! This was a little much for the church community. With all the "good" girls in their town, why did Joe want to choose Georgine? It was commendable that Joe had reached out to help this person in need. She deserved a chance at a decent life. They would help her get a job and dress appropriately and adjust to the social structure. But marriage? Really, that was going a little far, wasn't it?

The pastor officiated at a small, private ceremony, and things quieted down. Normally, when two singles in the church married, their social life changed dramatically. They were suddenly welcomed in homes that had never invited them before. But with Joe and Georgine, there was a hesitancy to completely embrace the new couple. No one openly rejected them, but they felt the sting of courteous reproof.

Georgine was very aware of the rejection and lashed out at Joe for the hypocrites in his church. Joe tried to soothe her. "Don't worry about what others think," he said as he cuddled her. "I love you totally, and that's all that's important."

Soon their attention was diverted by something more significant. Georgine was pregnant! The couple settled into a cozy three-bedroom house, and Georgine began preparing the nursery. Meanwhile, Joe's ministry started to take off. He was a charismatic Bible teacher. The youth group was growing, which pleased the church. Invitations began coming for him to speak in the area.

Shortly after the baby was born, Joe had his first invitation to speak in a nearby city that required him to be gone overnight. He couldn't wait to get back home and give Georgine a report. People were coming out in large numbers to hear him speak. Many were convicted of their sins. They were coming forward to make decisions to live for God and to live moral lives pleasing to Him.

Life was good for the next couple of years. Their first child, a boy, was born healthy. Joe received more and more invitations to speak. A Christian publisher even approached him about writing a book. These were exhilarating times. Joe didn't see the warning clouds starting to roil up like an angry thunderstorm. Georgine was slipping into depression. She looked for baby-sitters more often. Her wardrobe was changing back toward more alluring clothes. Some in the church took notice, and there were whispers of disapproval.

Georgine got pregnant again, and Joe rejoiced at the news. But Georgine wasn't so excited this time. There was definitely something wrong; Joe just couldn't put his finger on it. There were harsh glances from women in the congregation. He couldn't figure out why. And at home, Georgine became less romantic, rejecting his advances more and more frequently.

A daughter was born, and Joe was ecstatic. His ministry was thriving. By now invitations were coming from around the country. He was being asked to speak at major conventions of youth leaders and Sunday school teachers and teens. He was often gone several days at a time. But at home, things continued to deteriorate. It wasn't that Joe didn't try; it's just that nothing seemed to work with Georgine. She no longer seemed to care about his ministry. Even worse, she didn't seem interested in the children, either. Her eyes seemed to be wandering, but looking for what? Pangs of fear stabbed at Joe, but he repressed them.

One evening Joe came home from a weeklong speaking campaign. It had been a grueling week and a long trip home, including an hour-long drive from the airport. At one time, Georgine would have warmly welcomed him at the door. But this evening, he could see her sitting at the kitchen table, cradling a cup of hot tea in her hands.

"Hi, sweetheart. I'm home!" he yelled from the foyer, trying to hide his weariness.

There was no response.

Joe set his suitcase down, went into the kitchen, and put the kettle on the burner to make himself some decaf coffee. "Georgine, what's wrong?"

"Nothing, I suppose. Just that I'm pregnant."

"That's wonderful!" Joe exclaimed. With steaming cup in hand, he sat down opposite her. "When are we due?"

"We?" she said absentmindedly. She gave a date.

Warning bells went off in his head. Something was wrong, but what? It didn't hit him until later that night as he lay awake next to his wife. They had rarely been intimate during the past year. A simple calculation and he knew—he wasn't the father!

Joe cut way back on his ministry in anticipation of the birth of the third child. There were talks and tears. Joe made it clear that he loved Georgine. This would be their child. But Georgine didn't seem to care. She did seem to want more things. She spent money on jewelry, clothes, cosmetics, and her hair. Joe heard warning alarms as he looked at the new clothes hanging in their closet— they were becoming more and more risqué. A friend in his men's group pulled Joe aside one morning after breakfast and said, "You need to know—" He hardly knew how to say it. "Georgine's been seen around town with a couple of other men."

Joe was honest. "I've suspected. But what do I do?"

One thing he was certain of was that he should stop all travel.

He needed to be home. With Georgine showing in her pregnancy, she also seemed more willing to stay home. But there was still a distance that Joe couldn't bridge. He knew he'd lost her.

Shortly after the third child was born, Joe came home from work to find a baby-sitter and a letter. "Don't come looking for me," she wrote. "I'm going far away. Please don't take this too hard. You're a good man. You don't deserve me."

Joe wanted to scream. He knew what this meant. Georgine was returning to her old life, to men who cared nothing about her, who would abuse her, throw a few bucks on the nightstand, and walk away. Anger boiled within. How could she reject the one man who had truly loved her?

There was another problem emerging. The church elders had ordered him to appear at a specially called meeting. He suspected that what they wanted to say wouldn't be encouraging. He arranged for the kind old woman who'd taken in Georgine a few years ago to look after the children that evening.

The meeting was tense. The pastor seemed the most understanding, but he clearly wasn't in control of this meeting. After laying out the concerns, the board chairman came to the point. "The question we're wrestling with is how we can allow you to remain in ministry."

Another board member interjected: "We're concerned about the message it would send to our young people."

"We know how the teens love you," said another. "But the Bible is clear about our ministers being above reproach."

"I've done nothing wrong," Joe meekly said.

One board member immediately jumped in. "I always thought that girl was trouble. I never understood why you married her. From day one I said she wasn't right for this church. We should have done something—"

"You don't know what you're talking about!" Joe interrupted.

The pastor was next to him. "Keep calm," he said, patting Joe's arm.

"No! I can't!" There was silence in the room. "You think I don't know how you feel about Georgine. I know! I see it in the disapproving glances at church. In the unspoken words. In the invitations no one extends to us. We're an embarrassment to the church.

"Well, let me set the record straight. I love my wife. In fact, she's the only woman I've ever loved. I know that's hard for you to believe. I also can see what's going on in this church. Sure, this congregation looks good on the outside. But we're covering up rottenness. I see how some of you treat your wives. I see how some of you are far more interested in business than family. I know many of you don't care about the down-and-out around you, the people from broken homes, those who are sexually and physically abused. But when I reach out to love one of those people who has known nothing but abuse all her life, you judge her instead of encouraging her and welcoming her into our fellowship."

When one of the board members tried to interrupt, Joe raised his hand to stop him and continued speaking: "I'm not finished! I know the secrets many of you are hiding. Some of you are addicted to pornography. Oh, you cluck your tongues that I'm in love with a woman who is a prostitute, yet you lust after women who aren't your wives, and you devour magazines and videos and Internet sites that portray the vilest pictures.

"You have no idea how agonizing this marriage has been. You have no idea how painful it is for me to love someone with all my heart, knowing that she rejects me and the One who loves her more than any human being, and instead runs to those who abuse her. I have only loved one woman in my life, and that's Georgine. God has revealed to me that my love for my wife is a picture of how much God loves His church. God loves you, but you only pretend to love

Him. You don't understand my marriage because you don't see that my wife's rejection of me is exactly how you have rejected God!"

There was a collective gasp in the room. The stunned men couldn't believe this man would challenge their faith. Joe couldn't stop now. "That's right! My marriage is a judgment against you. God loves you, and yet you go after other loves. In the Old Testament, Israel went after idols. Today, you chase after idols of money, power, and lewd images, and in the process you turn your backs on God."

Joe managed to live off his savings for a year before the reality hit that he would have to find work of some kind. But if he went to work, what would he do with the children? They were still reeling emotionally from their mother's abandonment. As Joe wept and prayed, he yearned for Georgine. He still loved her, and the children needed her. *I need to show my love to her again*, he thought, recognizing the nudging of God. He called the kind lady who had helped him before, and he asked her if she would stay in his home to look after the children until he got back.

After she'd settled in and he'd hugged and kissed each child, Joe drove to the bank and removed the last few pennies that remained in his account. Then he drove to the distant city he'd gone to several years before. Somehow, he knew he'd find her there again. The search went on three days before he saw her leaning on the arm of a pimp. He spent another day observing how she was living with this man, who was hustling to get her business of the vilest kind. Finally, when Georgine wasn't around, Joe approached this man.

It wasn't easy to start this conversation, but he had to begin somewhere. "The woman I've seen you with, Georgine?"

"I don't know no Georgine," the pimp sneered.

"Well, I've seen her," and he described his wife.

130   your
m a r r i a g e
masterpiece

"Oh, that's Lila," he laughed. "So you want her, do you? Well, it will cost you."

"She's my wife."

"She's what?!"

"My wife. And I want to take her home. Her children need her."

The pimp looked at Joe, incredulous at his boldness yet also thinking of how to profit somehow from this situation. "Can't let her go. Not without remuneration. She's cost me a lot of money, and I have to make it back. You understand."

"I understand. How much do you need?"

The pimp named a price. Joe pulled out the cash, all the money he had left, and counted it out. It wasn't enough.

"What else can you accept in lieu of cash?"

The pimp took Joe's watch, a college graduation gift from his father, then pointed down the street. "She's in apartment 201," he said. "It's unlocked."

Joe hardly recognized his wife when he entered the apartment. She was sitting on a worn-out couch. She'd lost many pounds and looked anorexic. Georgine looked up at him but hardly seemed to recognize him. "I'm taking you home," Joe said kindly.

She turned her head away. "He won't let me go," she whispered.

"It's all arranged," Joe quickly answered. He knelt in front of her and gently took her hands in his. "Come home and live with me. You must give up this life of prostitution. I will take care of you and love you." Then he carefully helped her to her feet, held her in his arms, and led her downstairs to his car.

13

The One-Sided Marriage

Ted* was a friend in college. I respected him as much as I did any of my fraternity brothers because of his ability on the football field, his intelligence in the math classes we took together, and his desire to serve God. We teamed up in a campus outreach ministry during our senior year, and we had many encouraging talks about the future of our ministries while playing golf. Shortly after we graduated from college, Ted married Laurie*, his high school sweetheart, and the two of them signed up to work for an international campus ministry. Ted and I went to different parts of the country, but we stayed in touch through mutual friends.

A couple of years later I heard the news that Ted and Laurie had a baby girl. About the same time, Ted had grown restless and decided to attend seminary. He took a job driving a bus to help pay for tuition, rent, and groceries. Laurie was supportive of Ted's decision. She had already tasted a successful career and was able to use her skills part-time from home to help support the family. She never saw the crisis developing inside Ted.

What Laurie didn't know was that Ted was terribly insecure

about money. He'd grown up in a low-income family that constantly worried about making ends meet. He struggled with jealousy as he saw his friends have nice things his parents could never afford. Privately, he was determined that he would never suffer in this way. His frustration boiled over one evening when he told Laurie, "I will do anything for the sake of money."

Laurie was flabbergasted. "Do you realize what you just said?"

Coldly, Ted answered: "Yes, I do. And I mean it. I will do anything for the sake of money. I will not suffer the way my parents suffered. If I'm going to be a pastor, a church will pay me what I'm worth. Otherwise, I'm finished with ministry."

Once Ted's secret was out in the open, this marriage spiraled downward. Laurie could only watch in horror as her husband began pursuing his real dream of financial wealth. He quit his driving job and took a job in a marketing firm. He had a natural knack for business and was quickly promoted. Soon he was too busy for seminary, so he quit school to devote his full attention to business. A computer manufacturing company learned of him and quickly hired him to manage their sales and marketing. The company offered to pay all moving expenses for him and his family. That's when he dropped the bomb on Laurie: His family interfered with his career. This was too important for him. "Don't worry. I will support you until our daughter graduates from college. But you aren't coming with me."

I wish this tragedy was unique, but unfortunately it isn't. Laurie lived a nightmare for two years while her husband abandoned her emotionally for his true love of money and power. During that time, she was a model of Christ's love to all who knew the situation. She prayed fervently that Ted would come to his senses, but he never did. In some ways, it felt merciful that he finally left her rather than pretend they had a real marriage.

Unfortunately, many men and women live for years in marriages that are totally one-sided.

Hosea—Wimp or Hero?

For centuries, God endured a miserable, one-sided marriage. How bad was it? God gave us a taste through the life of the prophet Hosea. It was his story that I attempted to retell in a contemporary context in chapter twelve. Joseph is one of the translations of the name Hosea, and his story is God's story in a nutshell.

Just as we probably would view the story of the previous chapter as a scandal in our churches, so Hosea's story was a scandal in the Old Testament. I've wondered why God would ask Hosea to marry a harlot, and after she'd betrayed him, to go back and purchase her freedom. It seems utterly unfair that this man should have to suffer so much because of God's agenda to communicate His message to Israel. Surely God had other, better options available.

Some of God's instructions to Hosea actually violated Mosaic Law. It was highly unusual that a man would marry a prostitute in that culture, though that wasn't against the law. However, once Gomer was married and then committed adultery, by law she was condemned to execution by stoning.[1] Yet God ordered Hosea, "Go, show your love to your wife again, though she is loved by another and is an adulteress. Love her as the Lord loves the Israelites, though they turn to other gods and love the sacred raisin cakes."[2]

I don't know who I pity more, Gomer or Hosea. They both seem rather pitiful. Gomer gains a taste of genuine love, and what does she do? She spurns it! She exchanges a solid home life for a life of degradation. But Hosea seems like a wimp, letting his wife leave without a fight. And she returns only because he bought her like a slave. It wasn't his idea to rescue her—it was God's!

On the other hand, perhaps Hosea was a hero. Could I honestly say I am so willing to please God that I'd allow my heart to be broken? I can't imagine that Hosea's life was happy. Still, he could have ignored God's instructions and pursued his own idea of fulfillment. Instead, Hosea allowed his marriage and family to be used by God to reveal His heart. For Hosea, there was apparently more to life than personal happiness.

This is where I am forced to wrestle with the toughest cases of marriage. If personal happiness is our right in marriage, then how long do we hang on if we're not happy? The story of Hosea makes me feel like Peter must have felt when he asked Jesus, "How many times shall I forgive my brother when he sins against me? Up to seven times?"[3] I'm sure Peter felt very righteous, for tradition required only three times. But Jesus answered, "I tell you, not seven times, but seventy times seven."[4] By that Jesus was saying, "There is no limit to forgiveness." Hosea forces me to ask if there is any divine limit to what someone must endure in a marriage.

The most obvious type of one-sided marriage is that in which one partner is faithful and the other is not. This was the situation God faced with Israel. But there are other kinds of one-sided marriages. Several years ago, my local newspaper carried a front-page story about two marriages. In both, the husbands suffered a debilitating event—for one a tragic fall down the side of a mountain, for the other a stroke—that left them permanently disabled and their personalities changed. In both cases, the wife was left to pick up the pieces and care for her husband.

One wife stuck with her man. The other decided that as a "single" mother with a full-time career, caring for a handicapped husband was more than anyone could require of her. She insists she made the smart choice: "I would not have been able to survive in a situation where there was no hope. I needed to choose the healthy alternative, for myself and, secondarily, for others."[5]

So, who was right? Both cases seem unfair to the wife. Suddenly her life is turned upside down because of an event totally outside her control. Surely she didn't sign up for this, even if she did vow in an emotional moment many years before to love her husband "in sickness and in health." Does God really expect someone to endure such difficult circumstances? The answer from Scripture seems pretty harsh, unless I consider the fact that God has endured a miserable, one-sided marriage and has stuck with it.

I'm not talking now about blatant abuse. If a man beats his wife, she has a right to fight for the marriage by exercising tough love, and separation may be necessary. Nor am I saying that a spouse must endure endless infidelity—God showed us that was intolerable, again by exercising tough love. Jesus Himself acknowledged that adultery was the one legitimate grounds for divorce,[6] at least when the offender continues unrepentant. Even so, though God had grounds for divorce, He chose instead to fight for His marriage. The example of Hosea shows us the lengths that God will go to fulfill His covenant. Given His commitment to us, can I be any less committed to my spouse?

In many one-sided marriages there is no abuse or adultery. Perhaps one person simply wants a masterpiece of a marriage, but the other is apathetic or is unable physically or emotionally to return that love. Maybe the husband is just being a typical guy and doesn't understand or offer the sort of romance his wife craves in their relationship. What then? Or suppose a spouse has an addiction to drugs or alcohol, leaving the partner to endure many a lonely and anxious night. Maybe a husband gets himself hooked on Internet porn—there is no physical adultery, but the wife suffers because her husband is no longer with her mentally or emotionally. Or perhaps the husband is faithful to his wife, but she is unwilling or unable to give him the sexual pleasure he desires.

There is something mystical about a couple who endure and

triumph in a one-sided marriage. I'm in awe when I see it, as in the case of David and Vi Tillstrom.

Unable to Give Back

The community of Gresham, Oregon, still esteems David and Vi Tillstrom years after their deaths. Their son, Dave, says, "I can go into a store and be told, 'I just loved your mom and dad.' Dad was a good businessman. Everywhere I go, people who had business dealings with him talk about his integrity."

David and Vi met at church in the 1930s, and their courtship occurred around church events. They were married at the start of World War II and settled on farmland east of Portland, Oregon. Vi's physical problems began during the 1960s. She was occasionally forgetful or afraid to go someplace that had never bothered her before, though she usually managed to compensate. In the early seventies, she was diagnosed with Alzheimer's. There followed a long, slow deterioration that lasted many years. In time, as it became harder for David to care for his wife, family and friends encouraged him to place Vi in a nursing home. But in healthier times, the couple had promised they would never put the other in a retirement home or nursing home. They were determined to live together and die together in their own home. The realities of Vi's condition never changed David's thinking, even though by the early 1980s she could no longer speak and had to be spoon-fed as her weight slipped below 100 pounds.

Fortunately, David's business acumen had paid off, and as Vi slipped further, he was able to afford nursing care for 16 hours each day. The elder Dave always handled the graveyard shift. A hospital bed was placed in the living room, and Vi spent her days in that sunny room, surrounded by views of beautiful, lush farmland. At night, David would gently pick up his wife and carry her to his bed to sleep with her, telling her, "I love you, Vi." Though by now he was totally deaf, he was so attuned to her needs that he could awake in an instant to care for her whenever necessary.

I wonder how David Tillstrom felt when days turned into months, months turned into years, and his wife never got better. What kept him faithfully caring for a wife who was unable to talk to him or give him any affection? He was a man of few words, and I'm not sure he could have explained it. The younger Dave says that his father became a much gentler man during his wife's illness.

Dad was never a socialite. He was more into things. He bought and restored old cars. He knew how to make a wise deal on land—he was one of only a couple of farmers in the area who tied up water rights to his property, and that made him a fortune. But it really hurt when Vi got sick and after a while people from the church stopped visiting her. It bothered him because his wife had given so much to the church. "I can understand if they don't want to see me," he'd say, "but I can't understand why they don't want to see Vi." Well, I know it wasn't easy coming to see someone who looked like a victim of the Holocaust.

One day I was at the house and Dad said, "I'm going to do my missionary duty." I asked him what he meant, and he said, "I'm going to see some old people who can't get out anymore." Dad had come to realize what was really important—people were important, not things. He gave up much of his money because his wife was more important than his personal kingdom. I remember him telling me one night, "I'd give up everything I have if I could just talk with my wife again for two hours."

I believe that love kept Vi alive for many years. In fact, David ended up dying first from a brain tumor. His wife passed away just

138   your
m a r r i a g e
masterpiece

43 hours later. Though the sons obtained a nice inheritance, my friend says the real inheritance was the marriage of his parents. "They are a model that I want to copy in my marriage. It's one reason Mitzie and I know we are married for life, because of their example."

For nearly 15 years, this marriage was a picture of a one-sided relationship, where Mr. Tillstrom heroically gave himself to the care of his wife. Did the world notice? Maybe not. But the family and community sure did. His actions showed me the power of love and covenant. For me, their marriage was a masterpiece.

One Believes, the Other Doesn't

What does a person do when he or she loves God, and the spouse doesn't? The Scriptures address this situation, exhorting the believing spouse to remain married unless the unbeliever chooses to leave.[7] There are two reasons given. One is that, by the believer's staying, the unbeliever is "sanctified" by the believer. This means that as long as the couple are married, God can use the believing spouse as an influence on the unbelieving spouse. Perhaps the unbeliever will be brought to faith by the believing spouse.[8]

The other reason for the believer to remain married is that God is working out His plan: "Each one should retain the place in life that the Lord has assigned to him and to which God has called him." In other words, God is painting a picture—let Him finish it! There is no mention of the believing spouse's happiness. God seems to have a much higher purpose in mind.

There is one beautiful couple I know who have been married for more than 50 years. He came to faith in Christ about the time their children were full-grown. She has fully supported his choice while retaining her Jewish faith. Few couples are more devoted than they are.

Paul and Louise Peppin were married for 71 years. Early in their marriage, Louise came to believe in the claims of Christ, and for the rest of her years she faithfully attended church and communicated her faith to her children. But her husband didn't follow. He was a moral man who went to work after completing eighth grade. He provided well for his family but never prayed, never read the Bible, and only attended church later in life to help count the offering. Every single day, for 71 years, Louise prayed that God would bring her husband to the One she so dearly loved. But she died without seeing that prayer answered.

So, was it worth it? Did God hear this faithful woman's prayers, and if so, why couldn't she see the answer? I believe she did, but not from her earthly perspective.

One person whose life was deeply touched by Louise was her grandson, Bruce, who has served the ministry of Focus on the Family for more than 15 years. He personally witnessed "the rest of the story" after his grandmother died on Palm Sunday, 1994. Paul had suffered a series of strokes over the previous year and was in a partial coma. He could hear and open his eyes but was unable to focus his eyes or talk as he lay in the hospital. The family decided to delay telling him that his wife had passed away.

The day before the funeral, Bruce visited his grandfather. He sat by the bed and gently took his grandfather's hand. "Hey, Pop, this is Bruce. I've come in from Colorado."

The 93-year-old man opened his eyes, began breathing regularly, and listened intently.

"Pop, I know you aren't happy the way you are right now, but I know you can hear me. This next Sunday is Easter. It's the day we celebrate the Resurrection. Do you find hope that Jesus died, rose from the dead, and conquered death? Does this give you hope?"

Bruce didn't expect to see any response, but there was a small, noticeable nod of the head. Wondering if his eyes were playing tricks, Bruce again asked, "Pop, that's great! You know this Friday is Good Friday, the day Jesus died for us. But we have hope because He rose again. Do you find hope in that?"

Again, his grandfather nodded his head. Bruce felt a wave of gratitude. "Pop, I'd like to pray for you." Bruce then asked God, "Help my grandfather to know You are with him here in this hospital bed."

Two days later, after Louise's funeral, Bruce visited his grandfather again and was unable to rouse him out of the coma. They never talked again. But in that brief moment God had granted his grandfather one last opportunity to receive the message of eternal life. Bruce believes his grandfather had the same experience as the thief on the cross next to Jesus. "I believe my grandfather acknowledged all that he'd heard over the years and stumbled into the kingdom at the last hour. It's a legacy to the faithfulness of my grandmother."

Sure, Bruce's grandmother was in a one-sided marriage concerning the most important part of her life. But she clung to the fact that God had brought them together and that she had a part to play in a drama that was bigger than her individual happiness. Her grandson, Bruce, is part of that legacy.

Hope for the Lonely Hearted

So, what answers do we have for one-sided marriages? Do people simply have to endure them, without any hope of something better? One observation, based on Hosea and other portions of Scripture, plus the examples of people like David Tillstrom and Louise Peppin, is that God seems to highly value the obedient person acting in faith. When God told Hosea, "Go, take to yourself an adulterous wife and children of unfaithfulness," Hosea went and married Gomer. When Gomer violated her marriage vows and abandoned her family, God told Hosea to go and buy his wife back. There is no commentary on how he felt about this. He simply did it.

The heroes of Scripture are those men and women who obeyed God when it wasn't comfortable or easy. Abraham obeyed God and left his home to go to a new land, even though he didn't know where he was going. Esther agreed to go to the king and plead for her people, knowing it might cost her life.[9] Shadrach, Meshach, and Abednego refused to bow down to the image and stood up to the king, knowing they would be thrown into the blazing furnace.[10] All of them and many more obeyed God and did what was right, not knowing how it would all turn out.

In fact, while these three examples have happy endings—God made a covenant with Abraham; Esther's intervention did save the Jews; Shadrach, Meshach, and Abednego were saved from the blazing furnace—there are many examples in Scripture where there is no happy conclusion, at least from our limited human perspective. Near the end of Hebrews 11, nameless individuals are noted for their faith—people who were tortured or imprisoned or jeered at or in some way mistreated. The conclusion: "These were all commended for their faith, yet none of them received what had been promised."[11] The sad fact is that Scripture doesn't promise a happy ending here on earth for the person in a one-sided marriage. But to anyone who is obedient, there is a promise that God will be well pleased and will reward with these words: "Well done, good and faithful servant! You have been faithful with a few things; I will put you in charge of many things. Come and share your master's happiness!"[12]

A second observation is that it helps to concentrate on the big story. To the degree we recognize that we are part of a story bigger than us, we will gain some perspective on our situation. When happiness is the goal in my marriage, circumstances must cooperate, and when they don't, I'm frustrated. But if I realize I'm involved in a greater drama, it changes my perspective. Hosea realized that his marriage and family were being used by God as an object lesson for the people of Israel. I believe that realization gave his marriage meaning, and that was more important than his momentary happiness.

I think of Ted and Laurie in this context. She endured a hellish period of life married to Ted. But she was faithful to him and to their covenant. Though she fought for the marriage, ultimately she couldn't stop Ted from walking away. Twenty years later, all who know them both see Laurie as the heroine who is a godly light to Ted. He despised the light and chose darkness, but he knows what he rejected. I believe Laurie will hear the words "Well done." Meanwhile, Ted's friends pray for him. If and when he sees the light, I believe Laurie's faithful love will be a major reason.

I can't help but think of the example of Jesus, who on the night before His crucifixion begged His Father to remove the cup of suffering from Him. *Nevertheless,* He prayed, *not My will but Thine be done.*

I wonder if we might pray similarly. Laurie, David Tillstrom, and Louise Peppin might well have prayed this prayer: *Lord, I don't like this situation. I don't want to be in a one-sided marriage. Nevertheless, not my will but Yours be done.*

I can't pretend to think that such a prayer is easy for those suffering one-sided marriages. I understand why people want to escape from such situations. But are the only options to endure stoically or to escape? I think there is another option. In fact, I believe Laurie, David, and Louise all understood this intuitively. This is where the human marriage intersects with God's marriage, for the spouse has the opportunity to show a mate just how much God loves them. It may mean risking all of one's material possessions, as Hosea did. It may mean resigning a dream job for something that doesn't require constant travel away from home. It may require embarrassing oneself in the eyes of the world to let a wife know that she is the most important person in your life.

If God can take Hosea's marriage and make it a means of ministry to the nation of Israel, then perhaps He can use any marriage where one partner is willing to let God work. Because God isn't willing to give up on His marriage to Israel and the church, I believe He won't give up on any marriage where just one partner is committed to Him. God wants to make a masterpiece with whatever material He has. I can only conclude that means He wants to make a masterpiece of my marriage and of your marriage, regardless of their current condition.

If God desires to make my marriage a work of art, how can I refuse His invitation? But just what does that work of art look like? It's now time to gaze at the climax of the divine romance.

14

The Hero Saves the Day

Every story requires a climax. It's that moment when the protagonist must risk everything for his object of desire. God's desire was clear— He wanted the heart of His beloved. But she had been unfaithful to Him, and the price for her unfaithfulness had to be paid. By law, the price was death. But if she died, God lost what He most desired. There had to be some other way. The angels watched, but did they understand the drama playing out before them?

The stadium was full, buzzing with anticipation. Abdiel stood next to his friend Zephon, awaiting the great moment. They could hear and see Gabriel behind the "curtain," speaking to a group of frightened shepherds. "Do not be afraid," said the spokesman. "I bring you good news of great joy that will be for all the people."

"Do you understand what our Lord is doing?" Abdiel asked his neighbor.

"I know God is taking the form of a human," Zephon answered.

"Do you know why? What will this accomplish?"

"He loves the people. This is another way He can show them His love."

"It seems to me that He should reveal Himself to them in all His glory. Then they would see what we see and bow down and worship Him."

"Yes, they would indeed," answered the wiser Zephon. "They would bow down in terror. Notice how these shepherds cower before just one of us. How could they possibly bear the glory of the Lord?"

"But how can they recognize Him as a baby?"

"Hush! It's time."

The curtain rose and the angels could see the motley crowd of shepherds gazing at them as they began to sing. Abdiel had never sung harder. "Glory to God in the highest, and on earth peace to men on whom His favor rests." The music soared in the most astounding melody and harmony ever heard by human ears. Never had humans heard the angels sing, and Abdiel wanted this to be their greatest performance, to bring glory to God. When they finished singing, there was no applause from the shepherds. They were stunned. The curtain closed. The light went out, replaced by the stars in the clear, cold sky. For a moment, no one spoke. Then one of the shepherds said, "Let's go to Bethlehem and see this thing that has happened, which the Lord has told us about."

Like all the angels, Abdiel watched the growth of this unique child into manhood, but he couldn't grasp God's purpose for taking human form. If God wanted to reveal Himself to humans, then why didn't He come in glory as a king? There were moments when he thought the people were starting to see the picture. He especially cheered when the crowd wanted to make Jesus their king after He fed 5,000 with five loaves and two small fish. However, Jesus understood their intentions and escaped to a lonely mountainside.[1]

Abdiel groaned over the many disappointments he observed. The religious leaders seemed to oppose Jesus at every turn. When He became more explicit about who He was, many in the crowds rejected Him as well, leaving Him with only a ragtag band of disciples who staked their entire lives on His being the Messiah. Abdiel rejoiced as He watched the God-man raise Lazarus from the dead, causing many to believe in Him. Soon thereafter, Jesus triumphantly rode into the city as thousands cheered. Though he knew the prophet Zechariah foretold this event, still Abdiel would have preferred that the King be carried in an ornate coach rather than ride a donkey.[2]

Now he had just observed Jesus eat the Passover meal with His disciples, then lead them across the Kidron Valley to the Garden of Gethsemane, where Jesus separated Himself from the 11 and went off alone to pray. Abdiel was shocked by what he saw and heard and went looking for his friend. "Zephon, have you been watching?"

"Yes, it's terribly disturbing. There's a mob approaching right now."

Abdiel watched in horror as the mob entered the garden. He saw Judas come and greet Jesus with a kiss, signifying that this was the man who should be arrested. That was too much. "It's a trap!" Abdiel yelled, though the humans couldn't hear the angels' voices.

But Peter seemed to understand the situation. He drew his sword and swiped at the head of one of the crowd. The man sidestepped the blow, but the sword still clipped off the man's ear. Immediately weapons were drawn and a fight seemed imminent, but Jesus lifted His arms and with great authority in His voice ordered Peter, "Put your sword back in its place." The two angels listened eagerly as Jesus then said, "Do you think I cannot call on My Father, and He will at once put at My disposal more than 12 legions of angels?"

"That's right!" Abdiel yelled. "Call on us! We'll be there right away! We'll wipe them out in an instant!"

Zephon laid a hand on Abdiel's shoulder. "Calm down, my friend. There must be a reason He won't call on us. We must think."

Abdiel wasn't the type to spend time in reflection, especially with a situation that to him screamed for action. If only the God-man would call on him—there wasn't anything he wouldn't do for Jesus. But he also respected his friend, who possessed more understanding. So Abdiel stood and watched. And thought.

The pair observed as Jesus was bound and led to the high priest, and then before the Sanhedrin, where various witnesses brought accusations against Him. But there was no consistency in the testimony. So in frustration the high priest ordered Jesus to answer one question: "Tell us if you are the Christ, the Son of God."

All of heaven seemed to hold its collective breath.

"Yes, it is as you say," Jesus replied.

"Yes!" Abdiel exclaimed. "Now they'll get the message."

Jesus continued, "But I say to all of you: In the future you will see the Son of Man sitting at the right hand of the Mighty One and coming on the clouds of heaven."

"And we're coming with you!" yelled Abdiel.

Then the high priest tore his clothes and said, "He has spoken blasphemy!"

"What?" Abdiel couldn't restrain himself. "But it's the truth! How can there be blasphemy when He speaks the truth?"

Of course, no one could hear the angel's protestations. A contingent of soldiers marched Jesus over to Pilate, and the charade of justice continued. Abdiel and Zephon had to turn their heads as their Master was stripped and brutally scourged—the skin literally ripped off His back. They heard the crowd yell for Jesus to be crucified and turned back to see Pilate wash his hands and declare, "I am innocent of this man's blood."

"The governor knows Jesus does not deserve execution," Zephon said.

"Yet he allows it anyway," Abdiel muttered.

All of heaven watched as Jesus fell, trying to carry the cross to Golgotha. They watched as He stretched out His arms and allowed the soldiers to drive the spikes through His wrists. They watched as the cross was lifted up and then dropped into a hole, and the body of Jesus lurched forward, dislocating His shoulders. They watched, weeping now, as the crowd hurled abuse at the man who loved them.

Heaven was often a place of rejoicing and celebration. Abdiel had known the times of great joy Jesus had spoken of, when just one person repented of his sins and turned to God.[3] They had partied when Jacob yielded to the angel at the end of an all-night wrestling match. They had cheered when Rahab had sought protection of the spies in Jericho. They had praised God over the repentance of David following his affair with Bathsheba. They had laughed for joy when the Samaritan woman recognized the Messiah and revival erupted in Sychar.

But never had the angels known such grief. There was loss when they had to put down the insurrection and chase Lucifer and his rebels out of heaven. There was shock when God flooded the earth and wiped out all but eight members of the human race. But this was the ultimate tragedy. God had come to the humans in their own form, and they were murdering Him.

The angels could only watch in shocked disbelief as the God-man hung on the cross. Many couldn't bear it when they heard their Lord scream out, "My God, my God, why have You forsaken me?"

"Why? Why won't the Father rescue the Son?" Abdiel whispered to himself.

Finally, it was over. The body was removed from the cross, wrapped in nearly 100 pounds of linen and spices and placed in an empty tomb, which was a cave roughly hewn out of the side of a hill.

The two angels couldn't believe it. They walked away from their view of earth, wandering aimlessly. "We need to think," said Zephon. "There's a meaning to all we've watched. The Son even told His disciples this had to happen. God has a plan. But what is it?"

"I don't see how we can figure it out," Abdiel said. "If God Himself doesn't explain it, how can we understand?"

"I think He has revealed all that we need to know. Let's start at the beginning and see if we can find the pattern."

"By beginning, do you mean creation?"

"Yes. Do you remember what we saw on that wonderful day when the Creator molded the first man and woman?"

"We saw in the two of them a reflection of God Himself."

"That's right. But there was also the intimacy. God wanted to know these people, to walk among them, to interact with them, and gradually to reveal more of Himself to them. He's never done that with any other of His creation, even among us angels. Tragically, that two-way relationship was soon destroyed."

"I thought that was the worst moment of my existence. Until now! What were Adam and Eve thinking? They were told a lie—that they could be like God. What an impossibility! There is only one God."

Zephon nodded his head in agreement. "Lucifer wanted to be like God. That was just as ludicrous, even though he is many times greater than humans are. So, what happened next?"

"The humans multiplied, until there were millions of them. But with that increase in population came great increase in evil. The humans knew both good and evil, but they concentrated on evil all the time. Eventually it hurt Him too much to watch. He was sorry He'd ever made man."

"And so He decided to wipe them out, all except Noah and his family. I've sometimes wondered why He didn't eliminate them all and start over?"

Abdiel paused to reflect on that statement, then answered, "I've wondered, too, why He didn't create a new creature that would serve Him."

"We serve Him," Zephon reminded his friend. "I don't think the Creator wants more servants. Otherwise, He'd just create more angels."

"So, what does He want?"

"That is the great question, isn't it? Let's keep thinking. What's the next major event in human history?"

"God chose Abraham," Abdiel answered.

"Did you notice how tender He was toward Abraham? And Sarah as well? He treated them both with great respect. It was a little like Eden, as though He wanted to start over without completely starting over. He wanted someone who would willingly choose to love Him and be loved by Him. He still desired intimacy with humanity."

"So Abraham responded to God's invitation and left Ur and went to a new land of God's choosing."

"And what did God promise Abraham? A family. What do you need in order to have a real family?"

"Two people need to get married. God promised Abraham and Sarah a huge family."

"You're on the right track, but it's more than that. This wasn't just about Abraham and Sarah; it was about God and Abraham and Sarah. Do you remember Eden? That was a threesome—Adam, Eve, and the Creator. That was the difference. God entered into this marriage with Abraham and Sarah and became part of their family."

Abdiel meditated on that for a moment, then said, "I've thought a lot about that covenant ceremony you and I observed, when God promised to uphold the agreement for both of them."

"And He did! Remember, He told Abraham that his people would be strangers and slaves in another country for 400 years, but then God would bring them back to this land He'd promised to Abraham. He did all of that, using Moses, then Joshua."

"I understand that," Abdiel said, pacing thoughtfully. "And then God dwelt with them, first in the tabernacle, then in the temple. And He gave them laws to ensure that they were worthy to approach Him, because He knows no sin. But…"

"But it didn't really work."

"It seemed that God spent more time punishing His people than enjoying them."

"You know what's bothered me for a long time?"

"What?"

"God has said that He's a husband to Israel. But if these people are married to Him, it doesn't seem like much of a marriage."

"I agree! They fight constantly. She rebels against Him. He wants her love, and she seems intent on irritating Him. Why does He put up with it?"

"Let's go to the prophets."

"What do you mean?"

"Isaiah, Jeremiah, Ezekiel—all of them. Do you remember when God told Hosea to go and marry the prostitute? And when Gomer left him and went back to prostitution, Hosea went and bought her back as his wife."

"That still doesn't make sense to me."

"Then listen to what Hosea said to the people: 'The Lord has a charge to bring against you. There is no faithfulness, no love, no acknowledgement of God in the land.' And what did He accuse them of over and over? Adultery. Prostitution."

"Yet He refused to give up on her."

"That's right! Despite the insults and rejection, God pleads for her love. 'Return, O Israel, to the Lord your God. How can I give you up? My heart is changed within me; all my compassion is aroused.'"

"Okay, I understand that. It doesn't make sense, but I know that God for some reason absolutely desires these people. So how does the horror we just witnessed fit into this?"

"Do you remember what God commanded Hosea to do when Gomer left him?"

"The Lord told him, 'Go, show your love to your wife again, though she is loved by another and is an adulteress.' So Hosea went and bought her back."

"That's correct. He redeemed her. Before God sent Hosea to do that, three times He said to Israel, 'I will betroth you.' Do you know what that means?"

"It means He is committed to marry her."

"It also means He will pay the bride price—a payment to the bride's father. Hold on to that thought. There are two more observations we need to connect. First, remember the story of the great song of Solomon? How did the king win the Shulamite's heart?"

"By disguising himself as a shepherd."

"Did you notice how the God-man referred to Himself as a shepherd calling his sheep? I wonder if the reason He became a man was to win the people back to Him."

"Fascinating! Yes, that makes sense. I once asked you why He didn't simply reveal Himself in all His glory, and you said because they would be terrified. So instead, He came to them in disguise. What's the second observation?"

"In the final meal with His 12 disciples, Jesus said something I didn't really understand then. When He gave them the cup, He said, 'This cup is the new covenant in my blood, which is poured out for you.' Do those words mean anything to you?"

"Well, it was obviously a significant moment. But, no, I don't understand what those mean."

"Those are the same words a young man says to a young woman he wants to marry."

"Oh my!"

"First, the fathers negotiate a bride price. Once they agree, the young man pours a cup of wine and offers it to the young woman, saying he is willing to give his life for her. And by accepting the cup and drinking from it, she indicates she is willing to give her life for him."

The implications suddenly hit Abdiel, and he turned back to look at the tomb where Jesus was now buried. "He gave His life for His beloved?"

"I think that's the meaning," Zephon quietly observed. "But I think here the bride price has double significance. It goes back to the covenant ceremony with Abraham. You will recall that if either party violated the terms of the covenant, God promised that what happened to those animals would happen to Him. As you know, God's people have repeatedly violated the terms of the covenant. God can't ignore that. Before He can have His bride, payment must be made for violation of the covenant. Just as Hosea redeemed Gomer, so God must redeem His beloved. This is the bride price."

"So the Father sent His Son, and He's been sacrificed. By that He's proven His love. But…the price is so high. It's permanent!"

Zephon started chuckling, breaking the intensity of the moment. "I don't think so! There's another thing Jesus said to His disciples before that dinner broke up. He said, 'In my Father's house are many rooms' and 'I am going there to prepare a place for you. And if I go and prepare a place for you, I will come back and take you to be with me that you may be where I am.'"

"Isn't that—"

"Those are the words the engaged man says to his fiancée. Before their marriage celebration, he must go and prepare a place for them to live. Then he comes back for her and the wedding feast begins."[4]

Abdiel shook his head in wonder. "This is more than I can possibly take in. It's wonderful and baffling."

At that moment, there was a sudden explosion of sound all around them. Instantly, the two rushed with all the angels to see the tomb. One of their number had pushed the stone away.

15

The Heroic Marriage

My idea of a movie hero is someone like James Bond—a Renaissance man who can handle any weapon, drive any machine (be it car, plane, tank or submarine) with little or no instruction, and outwit the most devious criminal mind the producer can imagine.

If I were creating a hero, I would not have imagined Guido Orefice, the protagonist in an Italian romantic comedy that captured the hearts of millions of viewers, including me. Guido is a small, slender waiter who loves life. Dora literally falls into his arms one fateful day, and when their paths cross again in several unusual and hilarious ways, Guido is smitten by the woman he calls *principessa*, or "my princess." Dora is engaged to a stodgy bureaucrat, but Guido wins her heart and rescues her from a dreary future. They marry and have a son, and Guido fulfills his dream of owning a bookshop.

World War II forms the backdrop for this story, and at the start of the second half of this two-act drama, Germany occupies Italy. When Jews are rounded up, Guido, his elderly uncle, and his three-year-old son, Guisue, are taken by train to a concentration camp. Dora arrives home to find them gone and rushes to the station, where she demands to be put on the train with her husband, even though she isn't a Jew. The remainder of the movie is the story of how this family survives the horrors of the Holocaust.

The uncle and other elderly prisoners who are unable to work are taken to the gas chamber, and it is evident that all children in the camp will suffer a similar fate. To save his son's life, Guido concocts a story that all the people Guisue sees are participants in a huge game. The first person to earn 1,000 points wins, and the grand prize is a *real* tank, not like the toy tank Guisue left at home. So while other children are taken to the gas chamber, Guisue hides from the authorities. All of Guido's instructions—how to hide, to avoid the guards, to never complain—are designed to protect his son and are phrased as rules that will earn points toward the grand prize.

Though Dora and Guido can't be together in the prison camp, their love permeates the drama. Every thought and action is geared toward their ultimate reunion as a family. As the war nears its conclusion and the Allies approach the camp, German guards frantically destroy evidence of their horrific deeds. Prisoners are hastily herded onto trucks. Guido hides his son and searches for Dora to warn her not to get on a truck, which would be a death sentence. He is finally caught, and to save his son, he bravely marches to his own execution.

Just a few hours later, the prisoners are free. An American tank drives into the compound, and the joyful boy knows he has won! Guisue gets a ride on the tank, then has a jubilant reunion with his mother. The title of this film captures its theme: *Life Is Beautiful*.

Isn't it ironic that a story where the protagonist loses his life should feel so joyful? Americans rarely notice a foreign film with subtitles, but this movie transcended language and culture because it captured the sacrificial love that all of us, in the deepest corner of our souls, long to experience. Dora didn't have to get on that train,

and in fact, she was urged to go home, but she gave up her comfortable life to be near her husband and son. Guido literally sacrificed his life for his wife and his son. Both found meaning in life by
giving up their lives for those they loved. Both were heroes, and the
world celebrated by awarding this film three Academy Awards.

When it comes to depicting a hero, James Bond can't compare
with Guido Orefice. We may think we need a superhero with mighty
powers to rescue us from injustice, but what we really need are
everyday heroes who love sacrificially. That's why the gospel drama
is so powerful. The people of Israel were looking for a military hero
to rescue them from the Roman occupation. But Jesus had a higher
mission: to die for His beloved. Is there any love more powerful
than that? How can we resist such heroic devotion?

The Hero Makes the Right Choice

The Scriptures compare the first Adam with the perfect man, Jesus.[1]
It is at their points of greatest danger—for Adam, at the tree of the
knowledge of good and evil; for Christ, in the Garden of Gethsemane—that their dramas reach the climax. It's hard to appreciate
either fully when we already know the outcome. For a moment, it
helps to linger at the crossroads where each must make the critical
decision:

Will Adam, after listening to the serpent, accept Eve's invitation
to eat, or will he resist and try to save her?

Will Christ accept His Father's will and give Himself as the sacrificial lamb for His beloved?

Both Adam and Jesus face a choice: to heroically sacrifice himself for the good of the bride, or to take the easy way of escape.

The latter is the way of the coward.

The former is the way of the hero.

Adam chose the way of the coward.

158   your
m a r r i a g e
masterpiece

Jesus chose the hero's sacrifice.

Adam's choice gives me the excuse to take the coward's path in marriage.

Jesus' choice provides me with the opportunity to be the hero to my wife.

Why is this significant? Because in life, and especially in marriage, I am instructed to have the same mind-set as Christ. That counters my normal selfish tendencies to demand my rights, position myself to look better than others around me, attempt to manipulate people and circumstances out of ambition, or ensure that my physical needs are met, even if outside the bonds of marriage. When my wife sees someone acting this way, she observes, "He sure is full of himself." That is not a compliment.

In contrast, Jesus gave up His rights, His power, and His glory in submission to His Father in order to win our love. This is the climax of God's romance. This is where every marriage has a chance to reflect God's Masterpiece, which is the marriage of Christ and His church.

Two powerful passages of Scripture pull God's Masterpiece into daily life. The first is Philippians 2:5-8. For our purposes, I start it this way: "Your attitude toward your spouse should be the same as that of Christ Jesus;[2]

Who, being in very nature God, did not consider equality with
God something to be grasped, but made himself nothing, taking
the very nature of a servant, being made in human likeness.
And being found in appearance as a man, he humbled himself
and became obedient to death—even death on a cross!

The phrase "made himself nothing" can also be translated "emptied himself."[3] The selfish man is full of himself. Jesus Christ emptied Himself. A selfish marriage consists of husband and wife demanding their own rights. The heroic marriage reflects Jesus Christ, who gave up His rights as deity. The selfish spouse insists on being served. The humble spouse becomes a servant.

The second passage is one that makes most preachers tremble: Ephesians 5:22-33. I'm sure I've heard at least 50 messages on this passage and read many more explanations in books. Almost all such teaching explains in a matter-of-fact way the roles and responsibilities of husband and wife. But I never truly considered this passage in light of the grand romance between God and humanity. Now that I understand the Masterpiece, I wonder if I will view Paul's instructions in a new light.

> Submit to one another out of reverence for Christ.
>
> Wives, submit to your husbands as to the Lord. For the husband is the head of the wife as Christ is the head of the church, his body, of which he is the Savior. Now as the church submits to Christ, so also wives should submit to their husbands in everything.
>
> Husbands, love your wives, just as Christ loved the church and gave himself up for her to make her holy, cleansing her by the washing with water through the word, and to present her to himself as a radiant church, without stain or wrinkle or any other blemish, but holy and blameless. In this same way, husbands ought to love their wives as their own bodies. He who loves his wife loves himself. After all, no one ever hated his own body, but he feeds and cares for it, just as Christ does the church—for we are members of his body. "For this reason a man will leave his father and mother and be united to his wife, and the two will become one flesh." This is a profound mystery—but I am talking about Christ and the church. However,

each one of you must also love his wife as he loves himself, and the wife must respect her husband.[4]

It seems ironic that sermons and books on the Ephesians passage concentrate on the roles—wives submit, husbands lead. Those roles are certainly there. But I am struck with this fact: Both the husband and wife are instructed to follow the example of Christ! Jesus is the model for both headship and submission.

The Picture of Heroism

Take, for example, these words: "Submit to one another out of reverence for Christ. Wives, submit to your husbands as to the Lord." Our culture hates the word *submission*. It goes against human nature to be humble and submit to anyone, especially to a husband who may be difficult to respect. Submission is considered demeaning, and in one sense the culture is right. It is demeaning. I read again from Philippians 2:5–8:

- Jesus Christ…made himself *nothing*.
- He took the very nature of a *servant*.
- He became *obedient* to the point of death.

The most glorious God of creation, submitting to His Father's will, gave up all His rights and privileges and glory as God. Isn't that demeaning? Absolutely! But He did it willingly in order to serve a spouse who didn't deserve His respect. God asks us to do likewise, not for our personal fulfillment but to reflect His heart. That's why husband and wife can submit to one another. That's why a wife can submit to her husband.

My wife submits to me by honoring me in my role as husband, by supporting me in front of the children, by following my lead as the visionary trying to sense God's call in our lives and ministry. But I also submit to Jo, deferring to her expertise regarding the daily care and nurture of our children, the daily management of our budget, and the look of our home.

Submission is not about subjugation. I do not demand Jo's submission; she willingly follows the apostle's instruction because she loves the Lord and respects her husband. She knows I do not lord over her but value her unique gifts and her wise input in every area of our life together. I may have responsibility to be the head of the home, but like any good manager, I highly value all that my wife brings to our family. It makes me mad when I see women emotionally or physically abused in the name of submission, for that is totally counter to the example of Christ.

A husband is instructed to follow Christ's example, for that is how he can truly love his wife. I might "translate" the instructions of Ephesians 5 to husbands: "Al, give up your rights and be the hero to your wife, just as Christ was the hero to the church and gave Himself up for her."

We know what heroism looks like. From the soldier who throws himself on a live grenade to save his buddies, to the daughter working 16-hour days to care for her aging mother, at the heart of every hero is self-sacrifice—laying down one's own life for another. When God entered human history and sacrificed His life to redeem ours, He was carrying out the most heroic act of all time. In the process, He modeled what it means to have a heroic marriage.

The example of Jesus forces me to make a choice. Will I do what feels good, what I think will make me happy? Or will I do the right thing and take whatever courageous action is necessary for the good of my marriage?

One day at Focus on the Family, I received two touching e-mails. One was from a pastor who told me how he came home one Saturday to find his wife weeping. She confessed that she had had an affair with a man at work. She didn't see how her husband could forgive her. Naturally, he was angry, but he also knew how much God had forgiven him for his sins. How could he not forgive his wife? He had committed to love her for life.

The next day I received an e-mail from this pastor's wife. She told a more complete story about how she had suffered through a difficult childhood, come to faith in Christ, then married a nonbeliever, who then came to faith in Christ and felt called to ministry. Her husband was busy as a youth pastor while she worked a job to help make ends meet. At work, she became emotionally attached to a fellow employee, which led to the affair. She was so wracked with guilt that she finally confessed. "There were no words to describe the pain that my husband felt," she wrote. "There was talk of divorce, and he had every right to get one. But God told him to forgive."

This man decided to fight for his marriage. It was a terrible battle, because his wife was emotionally ensnared. She wanted to keep her job, but that meant working in close proximity to the fellow employee. She finally yielded to the Holy Spirit and her husband's tough love. Both husband and wife changed jobs and moved to a new home. This humbled woman concluded: "It was never in God's plan for this affair to happen, but I do believe that God used this dreadful sin to open my eyes. I have learned so much about God's grace and forgiveness. I thank God for a husband who is so close to the Lord that in the middle of all his anguish, he picked up the gospel and ministered to his closest disciple, his wife."

I thank God for this pastor, the hero in a marriage that could easily have ended up as another divorce statistic. I wonder what fulfillment he will have in time because he didn't give up but worked through his anger and fought for his wife.

The Meaning of Marriage

This example of a saved marriage gives me a tangible glimpse of God's love for humanity. God wooed His beloved, but she betrayed

Him. Yet God never gave up on that relationship. His marriage was so important that He paid the highest price possible to have it—He sacrificed His life for His bride. Why did Jesus do this? Because doing it made Him happy? No! The agony He suffered in Gethsemane conclusively shows how distraught this sacrifice made Him. He endured the suffering for His *future* happiness. This is the conclusion of Scripture: "Let us fix our eyes on Jesus, the author and perfecter of our faith, who *for the joy set before him endured the cross, scorning its shame*, and sat down at the right hand of the throne of God."[5]

Jesus wanted a bride—the church. He couldn't have her without being the hero. He didn't enjoy being the hero, but He did it for the joy He knew would eventually be His.

Is marriage about happiness? Yes, but we don't gain it by demanding it now. We don't obtain it by insisting on self-fulfillment in the relationship. Expectations that my spouse will make me happy inevitably lead to disappointment.

The Masterpiece Marriage of God with Israel, of Christ and His beloved church, brings me to this conclusion about the meaning of marriage here on earth:

MEANING IN MARRIAGE IS NOT FOUND BY
PURSUING HAPPINESS OR SELF-FULFILLMENT.

MEANING IN MARRIAGE IS DISCOVERED
BY PRACTICING SELF-SACRIFICE.

I wish I'd been able to communicate this to Jim in terms he could understand. Every athlete desires to be the hero at the critical point in a championship game. As a boy, I dreamed of hitting the game-winning home run in the seventh game of the World Series. It's a fantasy every boy has—the sport or other activity may vary; the dream of being a hero doesn't.

Unfortunately, few athletes get the chance to be the hero in the Super Bowl, World Cup, or Olympics. But every man can be the hero in his marriage—he can lay down his life for his bride. Every woman can also be the heroine by submitting to her husband as to Christ.

David Tillstrom was a hero to his friends and family, and to me, by caring for his invalid wife for 15 years.

Louise Peppin was a heroine by praying every day for Paul, and by submitting to him and honoring him. Her grandchildren rise up today and call her blessed.

Of course, for many of us, the heroic marriage isn't lived out in such dramatic circumstances. Yet Christ's example is for all of us. How does this play out in daily life? In much the same way it happens for an athlete. If a team wants to win a championship, every player must sacrifice daily by training and following the coach's instructions.

I have numerous opportunities every day to give up what I want to do and instead serve my wife. In this way, I glorify God because my sacrifice is a reflection of His heart and how He loves His bride. I've finally realized that my marriage is satisfying to the degree that I daily sacrifice myself for Jo's good. What does that mean?

It means biting my tongue when I would rather defend myself against something she said.

It means hugging her when she says she's feeling tired rather than asking her if she's taken her vitamins lately.

It's getting up in the middle of the night when a child cries rather than pretending I don't hear anything.

It means putting down my reading material and really listening when she wants to talk.

It means taking over some chores when she's got a hectic day.

It means cleaning the kitchen Sunday evening rather than leaving the mess for her to face on Monday morning.

It means that when I am accidentally exposed to porn while channel surfing in a hotel room far from home, I shut off the television because I won't allow any impure thoughts to invade my marriage.

One of the original purposes of marriage as God intended it in Eden was to reflect His image. That means marriage is about something bigger than the two of us. Marriage is one of God's primary means of speaking to the world, and the world does take notice when a man truly loves His wife the way Christ loves His church.

An athlete doesn't enjoy the pain of serious training. But he trains for the future reward of winning. This is the challenge for marriage—to sacrifice my momentary definition of happiness for the long-term good of my spouse, thus reflecting God's heart and earning His praise, "Well done, good and faithful servant."

Marriage becomes a masterpiece when I choose to surrender my selfishness and give myself to my wife. That is a daily challenge. But as hard as it is for me to love as Christ loves, I think wives have a harder job submitting to their husbands as to Christ. I can think of many an evening when I've thanked Jo for preparing another wonderful meal, and she has said, "I didn't feel like fixing dinner tonight." What compelled her to do it? Sure, she knows that her husband and family expect it. But it is also her sacrifice for Christ.

Jo accepts primary responsibility for the day-to-day care and nurture of our three children, staying on top of details about school and making sure their physical and emotional needs are met.

Several years ago, after several trips caused me to miss paying bills for a couple of months, Jo took over that responsibility and has done a better job of managing our finances than I did.

I have an amazing ability not to see what needs to be done

around the house. My wife finds an unending list of work to do, and I sometimes have to remind her that it's okay to let some things slide.

I wish I could say we succeed in always loving each other sacrificially. Of course, we fail often, but one consolation is that we are in the game. Every athlete knows he can't be a hero unless he is actually playing in the game. Every day Jo and I have new opportunities to demonstrate sacrificial love, and when we fail, our covenant reminds us that the next day we have a chance to try again to get it right.

Either Spouse Can Be a Hero

My friend Jim lost his chance to be a hero to Bonnie. Sure, it would have hurt to end his dream of playing major league baseball. But suppose he had said, "Honey, you have sacrificed for five years as I pursued my dream. I am willing to settle down so you can have your dream of a home and family." Or think how would she have responded if he'd said, "Bonnie, would you give me one more chance to try and make it to the major leagues? If I am not there by the end of this season, I will retire and we'll settle down." How would Bonnie have responded to either of those scenarios? I believe she would have responded with willingness to her husband's sacrificial love.

We need heroes today who will stick with their marriages and sacrificially demonstrate their love. A few years ago, I started meeting weekly with a group of six men from my church for Bible study and prayer. One of the men, Ron Luck, was about 10 years older than I. He exuded a joy that immediately made me want to know him better. Then, after about two months, Ron announced that he had accepted a job offer in Wisconsin. I was disappointed that I wouldn't have a chance to get to know him better. Just before he moved, Ron and his wife, Linda, visited our home, though Ron came disguised as Santa Claus—to the delight of my children. They looked like a wonderful couple who reflected the Masterpiece. Only later did I learn the rest of their story.

Linda was an extremely shy and insecure girl. At 17, she fell in love with Ron, attracted to his strength and bold personality. He treated her like a princess and made her laugh when they were together. So, when Ron popped the big question, Linda said yes, in part because she loved Ron but also because she saw marriage as an opportunity to escape a less than happy home. Not long after the wedding, Linda discovered that marriage can produce its own unhappiness.

Ron's assertive nature grew out of his own insecurities. While they were dating, it was attractive because Linda admired his strength. Once they were married, it became oppressive because she endured his wrath. The flame of Ron's temper could be ignited by the slightest hint of disrespect or disobedience. Linda often bore the brunt of a bad day on the job. The house was never clean enough. The kids were never quiet enough. All because Ron's life was not ideal enough. The family was constantly on edge, fearing the next explosion.

"I was a jerk!" Ron now reflects. "I was selfish, had a bad temper, and griped all the time. I never helped out when the kids were little. I was more interested in my own demands than Linda's needs." But today, after almost 40 years together, Ron and Linda's marriage is a reflection of God's Masterpiece. They love one another as best friends and life partners, and they are admired by many, including their now-grown kids and little grandchildren.

Through the years, Linda determined to overlook her own hurt feelings and unmet needs in order to give Ron what she knew he needed—support and respect. She did not do so because he deserved it. He didn't. She did it because it was the right thing to do. It was how she could model Christ's heroic sacrifice.

There was the time Ron wanted to follow his dream, selling everything to buy an old country store. A mother of two, Linda enjoyed the security of a steady paycheck. But Ron was unhappy in his work, and this was something he really wanted to do. So, resisting the urge to cling to what was safe, Linda became his cheerleader and business partner. She resisted the urge to complain during long days of hard work trying to make the store a success. When the business failed, she resisted the urge to blame, even though it took many years to recover financially.

Years later, when I met Ron, he felt trapped in a dead-end career. Linda, on the other hand, was thriving in a highly rewarding job. She had a good salary and the respect of colleagues. With the kids grown and friends nearby, Linda had never been happier or more secure. But Ron was offered a terrific job as vice president of marketing at Green Lake Conference Center. The look in his eyes told her that he needed this change, even though it meant a thousand-mile move. So, once again laying aside her own desires, Linda resigned her position and started packing.

Ask Ron and he will tell you that Linda is his hero. Why? Because of the countless times she gave up her own rights and expectations in order to support and respect a man who deserved neither. Because she modeled what it means to lay down one's own life for another. In the process, Ron's heart was changed and he is a better man today because of his wife's love. Linda turned a marriage that could have been a disaster into one that reflects the Masterpiece!

Suppose Linda had insisted on having her happiness? She could have ended her marriage years ago, but she would have missed the payoff today. My conclusion is that God doesn't ask us to do anything for our mates that He hasn't done for His bride. He asks wives to submit because He humbled Himself and served. He asks husbands to love sacrificially because He gave up His rights in order to love us to the point of death. The heroic marriage reflects the gospel itself!

I like Mike Mason's reflection on self-sacrifice and marriage:

> Marriage is the natural place to begin, and to practice daily, the curbing of our own freedoms wherever they prove offensive to the other person.... Who "wins" this battle of wills and whims is not the point; the point is that each tries to surrender as much as possible for the sake of the other so that the love between them may be honored and built up in every way.[6]

To have a heroic marriage, you must become a heroic spouse, whether or not your mate does likewise. There are no shortcuts, simple steps, or easy gimmicks. It requires the courage to overcome pride and selfishness in order to lay down your life for another. Not because your spouse deserves it; he or she may not. Not because it will improve your relationship; it might not. You do it because you are part of something much bigger than yourself, and because you are called to reflect the Masterpiece of God.

"Be imitators of God, therefore,...and live a life of love, just as Christ loved us and gave himself up for us."[7] The big question is *how* to do this. My initial reaction is that I can't be heroic. There are too many obstacles. My wife isn't always lovable. My selfishness is a powerful force compelling me to submit to my own desires. There are too many temptations—I can't possibly resist them all. Most challenging is the example of Christ—He was perfect! I can never live up to that standard.

Christ knew the problems we would face in our marriages, and that's why He didn't leave us helpless. Among His final instructions to His disciples, Jesus said, "If you love me, you will obey what I command. And I will ask the Father, and he will give you another Counselor to be with you forever—the Spirit of truth."[8] God, in the person of the Holy Spirit, provides us with all the help, wisdom, and power we need to be the husband or wife our spouse requires.

Because of Christ's heroic work, we can gain in our marriages much of what was lost in Eden when Eve and Adam ate of the forbidden tree. To illustrate, let's look at a picture of one couple who were heroes in the first-century church.

A Great Adv

Unlike Adam and Eve before the Fall, we do not live our lives in paradise. The reality of a fallen world assaults us daily. But what Adam and Eve once had and lost—a three-way relationship with God, a wonderful shared adventure, and a chance to reflect God's image and heart—has been restored by the heroic work of Christ. This vignette is my story of one couple, mentioned briefly in Acts 18 and in three of Paul's epistles, who experienced these three elements in their marriage.

The young man was breathless as he quickly entered a humble hut and shut the door. His wife of three years wiped her hands on her apron and turned to greet him. As she put her arms around him, she noted the worry in his eyes. "What's wrong?" she asked.

"We have to leave Rome. Now!" he answered, gasping for breath.

"Why so soon? I know the emperor decreed—"

"They're rounding up Jews. I saw soldiers just a mile from here. We don't have much time—an hour at most."

"Oh my!" the wife wiped her hands again and looked around

I'm baking bread. It will be ready in about 20

whatever we can get into one sack. You gather what-
will keep."

have dried figs and grapes."

The man was already packing a change of clothes for both of them. "Good. They are easy to carry. We have 50 drachmas. That should get us passage to Achaia and leave some for us to start a new business."

The woman worked quickly as her husband tied up their bag. "Have you thought about where we're going?" she asked.

"I was thinking we could return to Pontus, since our families are there."

"No, that would mean a trip across the province. Let's go to Corinth. There's a strong Jewish community there. With all the traders passing through, there should be ample business for a tent maker."

"Wherever we go, we must leave now!"

A few minutes later, the couple slipped out of their home and headed for the harbor. They could hear shouts and screams just a few streets away as soldiers swept through the homes of their neighborhood. They slept in the shadow of a ship, booked passage in the morning, and set sail in the early afternoon.

And so Aquila and Priscilla escaped the persecution of Jews under Emperor Claudius and settled in a two-room house in Corinth. One room was dedicated to the business; the other served as their living quarters. Aquila procured the supplies and did most of the manual labor; Priscilla handled the money and interacted with the customers. Priscilla was right about the opportunities for a tent maker. Soon there was enough business to move into a larger building and to hire several helpers.

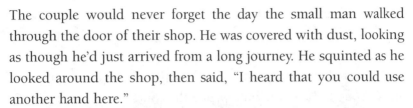

The couple would never forget the day the small man walked through the door of their shop. He was covered with dust, looking as though he'd just arrived from a long journey. He squinted as he looked around the shop, then said, "I heard that you could use another hand here."

Aquila nodded and acknowledged, "Business has been very good, and I'm behind on my orders. What is your background?"

"I grew up in Tarsus and apprenticed as a tent maker until my father sent me to Jerusalem to study."

"Jerusalem? Who was your teacher?"

"Gamaliel."

"So you are a Pharisee?"

"I was."

Aquila looked puzzled as Priscilla entered the shop.

The man introduced himself. "I am Paul. I'm looking for a place to stay. It's been a while since I plied my trade, but I work hard and perhaps I can help you with that backlog."

Aquila rose from his work and extended his hands in welcome. "Prisca, please get our guest some water so I may wash the dust off his feet. You are welcome to sleep here in the shop."

Priscilla returned quickly with a bowl of water.

"I will pay you a denarius for each full day of work," said Aquila as he washed his guest's feet. "For any new business you bring, you can keep half the proceeds, after materials."

"That sounds fair," said Paul. "Now tell me, is there a synagogue near here?"

"Yes, very close," Priscilla answered. "You will go with us on Sabbath. I will introduce you to Crispus, the ruler. I am sure he will invite you to teach."

That evening, after Paul had cleaned up from his trip, the three of them sat down for dinner. "Where have you come from on your journey?" Priscilla asked.

"I was in Athens for a few days and spoke in the Areopagus."

"Why? Were you on trial?"

"No. I debated a group of philosophers in the marketplace. They brought me to the hilltop, and the court asked me to present this new teaching. I got the impression that they love to sit around and listen to the latest ideas."

"Surely the Greeks know about the God of the Jews. This is not new," said Priscilla.

Paul smiled and leaned back as he said, "Then you have not heard of the man Jesus, who is the Christ!"

They talked late into the night, and Paul told them all about Jesus and how He was crucified and then raised from the dead three days later. The couple were thrilled to learn about the Christ and eagerly believed. Paul didn't need much urging from them to tell about the growth of the church and his adventures as he was sent from Antioch to Cyprus. He told how he then carried the Good News to both Jews and Gentiles in such places as Iconium, Philippi, and Thessalonica.

On Saturday the guest of Aquila and Priscilla preached at the synagogue to the community of Jews, who listened intently.

Paul was invited to speak on subsequent Sabbaths, but the tone of the meetings became acrimonious as many in the synagogue challenged Paul's assertion that Jesus was the Messiah. By the time Silas and Timothy arrived to join Paul in his work, it was obvious that the community of Jews was hopelessly divided. Paul stood in front of the synagogue and shook out his clothes in protest, shouting,

"Your blood be on your own heads! I am clear of my responsibility. From now on, I will go to the Gentiles."

With the arrival of his associates, Paul no longer needed to work, and he was invited to set up operations in the home of Titius Justus, who lived next door to the synagogue. There a group of believers gathered, including Aquila and Priscilla, and Crispus and his family. Paul still spent time with the couple who had welcomed him to Corinth, frequently partaking in a meal together.

At one of those gatherings, Priscilla observed to her guest, "You seem stronger this week."

"In what way, Prisca?"

"Last week you seemed afraid. Apprehensive. You were so bold in the synagogue, but after you moved next door, it seemed to me you were worried."

"You are very perceptive," Paul answered. "I was afraid. You smile—you think I am always so bold that nothing bothers me. But there is a pattern in every city I visit. I go to the Jews first, and a few believe, but the rest expel me from the synagogue. Then I preach to the Gentiles, and the jealous Jews cause an uproar in the city. In Lystra, they stoned me—"

Priscilla gasped.

Paul chuckled. "You didn't know that? Yes, I was dragged outside the city and left for dead. But the disciples cared for me. I could tell you about many such adventures. So in answer to your kind question, yes, I was worried. One doesn't look forward to being stoned or beaten. But the Lord appeared to me last night in a vision and said to me, 'Do not be afraid; keep on speaking, do not be silent. For I am with you, and no one is going attack and harm you, because I have many people in this city.' So I will be staying here for a while."

Paul lived for more than 18 months in Corinth. The church was established, though not without controversy. The Jewish community verbally attacked Paul and hauled him into court on charges that he was creating a new religion contrary to Roman law. But the proconsul dismissed the charges, viewing this as strictly an internal dispute within an established religion, which was of no concern to Rome. A few weeks later, Paul announced that he was leaving for Syria.

Priscilla lay sleepless on their bed, cuddled against the back of her husband. "I have a crazy idea," she said.

"Another one!" said Aquila, stifling a yawn.

"Now, I haven't led us astray so far, have I?"

Aquila rolled over to face his wife. "No, it was your idea that we go to Rome, and we did well there until the Jews were expelled. And we've done well here in Corinth. Every one of your ideas for the business has worked. So, what's this latest idea?"

Priscilla pushed herself up on an elbow and leaned her chin on her hand. "Have you thought about how fortuitous it was for us to land in Corinth?"

"Well, it is perfect for our business."

"I'm not talking about business. I'm talking about how we met Paul. It was as though God brought us here to meet him."

"Yes, I have thought about it. I feel God is no longer just the One we worship, but that He is somehow involved in our lives."

"That's what I'm feeling, too! So I've been thinking. Maybe God wants us to help spread this good news of Christ."

"How can we do that?"

"I think we should go with Paul! I've found someone who can run the business for us, someone we can trust. I've counted our savings, and we can afford to support ourselves for at least a year, maybe more. God is obviously using Paul, and I want to see what happens."

Aquila folded his hands behind his head. "Prisca, I love Paul as much as you do. But God can use us here in Corinth. Why leave when we have such a good life?"

"Because there is more to life than our business or our comfort. I think everyone should hear this wonderful news Paul has given us. But he's only one man. He needs help, and I think God wants us to go with him."

Aquila sighed. He never seemed to win any arguments with his wife. He didn't try this time. "Frankly, I've felt something similar in my spirit. Okay, let's talk with Paul and see if he will let us go with him."

The next day, the couple found their friend and proposed their idea. Paul was enthusiastic, and a few days later they sailed for Ephesus. Per his custom, Paul preached in the synagogue, and they asked him to spend more time there. But Paul said he needed to go on to Antioch. "I will come back if it is God's will," he said.

"We'll go with you," said Priscilla.

"No, Prisca, I think you should stay here in Ephesus. God can use you here."

Aquila noted, "I've been looking around. I think there's plenty of business for a tent maker here."

Paul liked that. "Yes, set up a business here. Talk about Jesus to all who come to your shop. Encourage those who believe. Draw on your experience in Corinth to help establish the church here."

So Paul left Aquila and Priscilla and sailed to Caesarea. The couple set up a tent-making shop in Ephesus, and soon a tiny group of believers were meeting in their home every Sunday.

One Saturday, Aquila and Priscilla attended synagogue and listened to the most compelling teacher they'd ever heard. He was an Egyptian who possessed a strong voice and spoke with great passion.

Apart from Paul, they'd never heard anyone with a better understanding of the Scriptures. "The prophet Isaiah foretold a great prophet who would come in the desert and announce, 'Prepare the way for the Lord.' Today, I tell you that this man has come! His name is John. Listen to his words!"

The Egyptian announced the good news that forgiveness of sins was possible "if you repent," and he urged the congregation to demonstrate the fruit of that repentance. With many examples, he explained the evidence of repentance: "If you are in business, don't charge more than a fair price. If you see a beggar, give to him what you can." The speaker closed his message with this bold pronouncement: "This man, John, is not the Messiah. But he points the way to One who is coming soon, the Messiah who will finish the work John began. Of Him, John proclaims, 'The thongs of His sandals I am not worthy to untie.' Let us prepare for the Messiah. Repent!"

It was a moving message, and Aquila and Priscilla couldn't wait to meet the speaker. It took a while before they could break through the crowd to the man named Apollos. Priscilla grabbed his hand and said, "You must come to our home for dinner!"

"I am staying with the synagogue ruler—"

Priscilla interrupted him, "You simply *must* come. We have wonderful news. The Messiah whom John proclaimed—the one you look for—He has come! We will tell you about Him."

As soon as it was sundown, Priscilla prepared a wonderful meal. Apollos showed up at their home with scrolls. After they ate, the three of them talked. "His name is Jesus, from Nazareth," Priscilla stated, unable to contain her excitement. "John recognized Him and saw the Spirit of God descend on Him."

Apollos listened intently. "Tell me everything. Don't leave out a single detail."

And so the couple told all they knew about the life, miracles, and teachings of Jesus. When they came to the last week of His life, their guest was riveted to every word as they told about the betrayal, the trial before the Sanhedrin and then before Pilate, and finally His crucifixion and burial. Apollos opened up one of his scrolls, and when he found the passage he was looking for, he read, "'He was pierced for our transgressions, he was crushed for our iniquities.... By his wounds we are healed.'[1] This is remarkable. It all makes sense. The prophets said this would happen!"

"But the story isn't over," said Aquila. "In fact, this is the best part."

"He didn't stay in the grave!" said Priscilla. "Three days later, God brought Him back to life. He was resurrected and His disciples saw Him. There are literally hundreds of witnesses to this!"

The great teacher kept his scroll open as he listened with amazement. His face glowed as the realization hit him. "That makes perfect sense. Listen to Isaiah! 'He will see his offspring and prolong his days.'[2] This right after the passage I read about His suffering. How could He see His offspring if God didn't bring Him back to life? And again Isaiah says, 'After the suffering of his soul, he will see the light of life and be satisfied.'[3] This is perfect! The prophets spoke of all this, but we didn't understand."

They spent most of the night talking, answering Apollos's questions as well as they could, until the oil of their lamp ran out and the predawn sky began to glow a deep red.

Apollos met many times with the couple and with the tiny group of believers over the next few weeks. Always he brought his scrolls with him and studied the Scriptures, finding many supporting passages that confirmed Jesus as the Messiah. He wanted to know where there were more believers, and the couple told him about the work of the disciples, especially about the itinerant teacher Paul. One evening, Apollos announced, "I feel compelled to move on. I must preach this wonderful news. I would like to go to Achaia."

"That's wonderful," said Priscilla. "Aquila and the brothers will write a letter of recommendation to the church in Corinth. I know they would welcome you."

Apollos boarded a ship for Corinth, and Aquila and Priscilla were full of joy as they returned to their home and business. "You know, Prisca, I don't believe there is anything more exciting than helping another to see the light."

Priscilla agreed. "Apollos is a gifted teacher. He can accomplish much more than we can. He will bring many to our faith."

Paul was gone a couple of years, and the church at Ephesus struggled, with only a dozen or so believers. It was with great joy that Aquila and Priscilla welcomed the apostle back to the city, and from the moment he arrived, activity increased dramatically in the region. It began with an outpouring of the Holy Spirit. People were so responsive that Paul set up a school for disciples, and believers from all over the region came to study. Both Aquila and Priscilla attended the discussions as often as they could without neglecting their thriving business.

These were exciting days. Miracles occurred—the sick were healed and evil spirits were cast out. Even more amazing were the many who came forward to confess their evil deeds. One memorable night, a number of converts who had practiced sorcery brought their scrolls and burned them in a gigantic bonfire. The value of those scrolls was estimated at 50,000 drachmas.

Soon after that event, Priscilla and Aquila invited Paul to dinner. Paul relaxed in their presence and talked freely from his heart. "You two are a remarkable couple," he said. It was almost midnight, and shadows flickered on the walls from the oil lamp on the table in their midst. Despite the late hour, none of them wanted this intimate time to end. "You are experiencing marriage the way God intended it to be."

"You mean God has a plan for marriage?" Priscilla asked.

"Absolutely. Remember, in the Prophets, God says He is the husband of Israel. Now God has reached out to the Gentiles and is bringing them into the family. His bride is the church. Your marriage, my dear friends, is intended to be an expression of this mystery, which is Christ and His church."

Aquila listened, trying to comprehend these strange words. Priscilla, in her typical manner, wanted more. "This doesn't make sense. God falls in love and gets married?! Surely the prophets spoke of marriage only as a metaphor."

"No, my dear Prisca, it's more than a metaphor. I'm just coming to understand this myself, but God wants a marriage between two believers to reflect the love He has for the church. For example, dear Prisca, you like to control things, and you are a wonderful organizer, but you need to learn how to submit more to your husband as unto the Lord."

Priscilla tried to interrupt him, but Paul held up his hand and continued speaking: "And you, Aquila, my dear brother, you need to learn to love your wife just as Christ loved the church and gave Himself up for her. Together, Prisca and Aquila, you are to be a picture to the world of God's love for us."

"It's not natural for me to submit to anyone!" Priscilla was intense but eager to understand.

"I am not telling you to stop being the people God created you to be. Prisca, God has given you wonderful gifts, and you use them well. But God has ordained the husband to be the head of the wife, just as Christ is the head of the church. Aquila, you are to love your wife just as you love your own body and feed and care for it. That in no way denies your wife's talents, any more than you would ignore the skills in your own body."

Aquila ventured a question that both he and his wife were thinking. "How does this work? I don't feel I'm naturally a leader."

"God provides the means," Paul answered. "Prisca, you can't submit in your own strength. And the kind of tender, sacrificial love God requires of a husband isn't natural. That's why you must be filled with the Holy Spirit. It is the Spirit who gives you the ability to fulfill your marital roles."

"The Holy Spirit was missing before you returned to Ephesus," observed Aquila. "I can see now that He is the moving power behind a vibrant church. But how does that work in our individual lives?"

"Have you ever seen someone drunk?"

"Of course!"

"A person who is drunk is filled with wine, and that leads to debauchery because the wine controls him. A Christian should not get drunk, but instead he should be filled with the Spirit. When you are filled with the Spirit, you will speak to one another with psalms, hymns, and spiritual songs. You will sing and make music in your heart. You will always give thanks to God the Father for everything. Prisca, the Holy Spirit enables you to submit to your husband. Aquila, you can love your wife as Christ loves the church when you are filled with the Spirit. Together, the Holy Spirit produces in you, through your marriage, a picture of God's love for His people."

The apostle laughed at the look on the faces of his friends. "You will understand. We are to be imitators of God and live a life of love. Marriage is the best place to learn this truth. 'For this reason a man will leave his father and mother and be united to his wife, and the two will become one flesh.' This is a profound mystery. I am talking about Christ and the church."

Aquila reached out and caressed his wife's hand, and together they sat silently, meditating on these incredible truths.

There were ominous rumblings in Ephesus. The growth of Christianity affected the city's major attraction, the temple of Artemis. It hit the silversmiths particularly hard, as many of the tourists and worshipers to the temple bought figurines of the great goddess and other souvenirs. One day a man named Demetrius gathered all the silversmiths and workers in related trades to protest that Paul and his converts were destroying their business.

Priscilla was at the market when the uproar erupted. She hurried home and found her husband. Together they ran toward the noise, and as they got close to the crowd, they heard people chanting, "Great is Artemis of the Ephesians!"

At the edge of the crowd Aquila shouted, "I see Gaius and Aristarchus! The crowd has them!" The two men were traveling companions of Paul.

"They're moving toward the theater!" shouted Priscilla.

The couple, using side streets, quickly made their way to the huge amphitheater built into the mountainside. Meanwhile, the crowd surged up the great boulevard, and by the time Aquila and Priscilla arrived, the theater was half full and angry citizens were streaming in.

A disturbance near the stage entrance caught their attention, and they hurried there to find Paul arguing with several of the leaders of the church. "I must speak to them!" Paul insisted.

"Don't go in there!" pleaded one of the men.

Priscilla and Aquila pushed their way toward Paul. He caught their eye. "There you are! You will understand that I must go in and speak to this crowd."

"No, it's suicide," said one of the disciples.

Some of the crowd recognized Paul and began screaming, "He's the ringleader!" The disciples formed a wall around Paul and moved him away from the entrance. Meanwhile, the roar of the crowd inside the amphitheater increased: "Great is Artemis of the Ephesians! Great is Artemis of the Ephesians! Great is Artemis of the Ephesians!"

"There's the city clerk. Let me talk to him!" Paul yelled, referring to an official who hastily made his way into the theater.

"I have a message from the province officials," said one of the disciples who had just run up to the crowd around Paul. "They plead with you not to go inside the theater. Let the officials handle this."

The crowd swarmed around Paul, who seemed intent on making his way through the stage entrance. Aquila glanced at his wife, who nodded and grabbed Paul by the arm. "Come quickly," she shouted. Aquila meanwhile pushed through the surging crowd to make a path for his wife and Paul. The angry citizens seemed intent on getting into the arena and ignored the threesome and a few of their friends making their way in the opposite direction. "Let's go down this side street," Aquila yelled.

Finally, they escaped the crowd. Behind them, they could see the theater was now full, and nearly 20,000 citizens of the city were screaming, "Great is Artemis of the Ephesians!"

Paul looked as though he wanted to return to the action, but the couple pulled on him and led him to their home. In the distance, they heard the crowd grow quiet, perhaps for a speaker, then erupt again.

It was several hours before a calm descended on the city. Paul asked for the disciples to come to the home of Aquila and Priscilla, where he announced that he was leaving. "It's time. You are well equipped to continue the work," he told the men and women crammed into the house. "I will leave at daybreak for Macedonia. I will be going to Jerusalem via Macedonia and Achaia. Then I must visit Rome."

As they parted, Priscilla, thinking of their escape from the city a few years earlier, said, "Rome will be dangerous."

"I know," Paul said. "But the church there is growing. I have longed to visit those brothers and sisters and to give them some spiritual gift to help make them strong."

Aquila then said, "Actually, I was thinking we should go back there ourselves. We have many friends. Maybe we can be of service to the church there."

Priscilla looked at her husband in surprise. "You haven't said anything about that to me."

"I've been praying about it, now that Claudius is no longer emperor," he said. "I was planning to bring it up to you and see what you think. Your ideas are still important to me."

"If God leads you two, then go!" Paul encouraged his friends.

The couple was back in Ephesus after spending several years in Rome, where a church met in their home. It was late evening when they heard a knock on their door. Aquila opened it. "Timothy!" he shouted. "Come in, my brother!"

Priscilla quickly gathered some bread and wine for their friend as Timothy said, "I have a letter from Paul."

When they were seated, Timothy opened the scroll and said, "He writes, 'Greet Priscilla and Aquila and the household of Onesiphorus.'"

"It's kind of him to remember us like that," said Aquila.

"When I'm with him, Paul often speaks warmly of you. He has told of how you helped him in spreading the gospel and building the church. He also tells about how you risked your life for him."

"He must be referring to the riot here. It was a dangerous situation, but I felt God was protecting us."

"Has Paul had his trial yet?" Priscilla asked.

"Yes, I'm afraid so. He writes, 'At my first defense, no one came to my support, but everyone deserted me.' He has asked me to come, and to bring his cloak and scrolls."

"You should not go by yourself. We will go with you," said Aquila.

"That is kind of you. But I think it is better if I go alone. I am younger than you and better suited for this trip."

"It sounds like he is discouraged," Priscilla said quietly.

"No. Tired, maybe. But listen. He writes: 'I am already being poured out like a drink offering, and the time has come for my departure. I have fought the good fight, I have finished the race, I have kept the faith. Now there is in store for me the crown of righteousness, which the Lord, the righteous Judge, will award to me on that day—and not only to me, but also to all who have longed for His appearing."

Tears streaked the faces of the couple who loved the apostle so. "We must follow his example," whispered Aquila.

Priscilla squeezed her husband's hand. "Yes, we must finish well," she answered. "God has directed our steps and used us and our home for His purposes. Our life together as Christians has been quite an adventure."

"Yes," agreed her husband. "By His grace, the adventure will continue until we, too, are ready to receive His reward."

17

Return to Eden

Jo and I have made it a practice to observe older couples, especially those married more than 40 years, looking for glimpses of the Masterpiece. One long-term marriage we admire is that of Fred and Gwen Landis. For six years we lived just two blocks away from this couple and saw them every Sunday in church. Theirs was a simple and sweet romance. They met while in college, though they were attending separate schools. Fred was a student at Albany College in Oregon and attended a small church where Gwen's father was the pastor. Fred and Gwen dated whenever she was home from Simpson Bible College in Seattle.

One evening, Fred wanted to kiss Gwen good night. With a twinkle in her eye, she informed him, "You can only kiss me on the cheek. I'm saving my first kiss on the lips for when I'm engaged."

A couple of years later, after her father took a pastorate in Seattle, Gwen visited a friend in Albany. Fred hurried over to see her between classes. The hour sped by. He stood up to run to class and leaned over to kiss Gwen on the cheek, but her mouth got in the way. He didn't think anything of it as he hurried back to campus.

The next afternoon, Fred called on Gwen. "You know what happened when you kissed me yesterday?" she said.

"No," Fred answered. "What happened?"

"We got engaged!"

"Really! Great! Let's tell everyone and make it official!"

They were married on October 20, 1928, at University Gospel Church in Seattle. Fred took a job at Simpson Bible Institute and assisted Gwen's father as visitation pastor. Gwen stayed home and kept house.

Soon after they were married, disaster struck. As a wedding present, Gwen's grandmother had given them a generous financial gift that they placed in a savings account. But after the stock market crash of 1929, their bank closed and never reopened. They lost all their savings.

Over the next 42 years, Fred pastored eight small churches in the Pacific Northwest. Gwen assisted him in the ministry, playing piano and organ, teaching Sunday school, calling on families, and visiting the sick.

Through the Depression, Fred and Gwen had four children—two sons and two daughters—and literally depended on God to meet their needs. The churches where they pastored in those years provided a parsonage and the often meager freewill offerings on Sunday. Gwen recalls that church attendees shared their garden vegetables. "In Wenatchee, we were given a lot of apples. And there was a woman who gave us a pot roast every week—we made it last several meals. If that was living from hand to mouth, it was from God's hand to our mouths!"

Fred and Gwen Landis were 102 and 101 years old respectively, and celebrated their 77th wedding anniversary in October 2005. Fred retired from the pastorate in July 1970, and since then they have lived in Salem, Oregon. Twice a month they participate in a special missionary prayer meeting at their church that includes several retired missionaries. "Prayer has been part of our life together since we first married," Fred explains. "When we had kids, we had family worship with the children after breakfast. Sometimes the neighbor kids joined us on the way to school. Since retirement, prayer is our life. Prayer is often a missing labor in the church. So that's our ministry for as long as God wants us to be here."

Gwen and Fred willingly talk about the richness of their marriage. "Tough times draw us together, not apart," Fred says. "We are committed to work together, pray together, plan together, play together. We're one. We do it all together."

What drew Jo and me to this humble couple? Actually, it was the little things. Their comfort with each other. Their meaningful glances. The times they acted like a young couple who were dating rather than veterans at marriage. I remember one night when Fred and I and the other elders of our church were spending a weekend at a lodge about a 45-minute drive from Salem. We were all relaxing, playing pool, and getting better acquainted when Fred stood up about eight p.m. and announced he was heading home. The rest of us were surprised, and I teased Fred that he couldn't bear to spend a night away from his wife. Standing regally erect at his full 6'3" height, he looked down at me and kindly informed me that as much as he enjoyed this company, he would much rather spend the night with his wife. At that moment, I felt tremendous respect for Fred.

For me, Fred and Gwen are a picture of marriage as God intended it. The world may pay little attention to this couple. Fred didn't pastor a megachurch. Gwen didn't record an album. They didn't build a huge business. "All" they did was faithfully love each other, raise four children, and serve God together. To the world, the marriage of Fred and Gwen Landis may be insignificant; to the church, it may be a tiny detail in God's grand design; but for Jo and me, this marriage is a painting of exquisite beauty—a glimpse of the incredible picture God longs to paint in every marriage.

Regaining What Was Lost

I believe it is possible to recapture what the first marriage had in Eden. Before the Fall, Adam and Eve enjoyed a unique three-way relationship with God. They had a clear mandate to fill the earth— an exciting adventure that also taxed the human mind, challenging the first couple to learn and grow in knowledge and understanding of God's creation. Further, in some mysterious way, their union was a reflection of God Himself.

All that was lost when Adam and Eve ate of the tree of the knowledge of good and evil. The magnificent image God intended for marriage was marred. Instead of a threesome, each giving to the others, marriage became a twosome, with each spouse primarily interested in having selfish needs met. The world was subdued, but often by force rather than by a benevolent ruler, and women were often kept out of the process. Knowledge grew slowly and often was detached from any recognition of the Creator. Husband and wife rarely made this a joint effort. In short, marriage became only a faint, murky image of what God intended.

When Jesus paid the bride price with His blood, and thus laid claim to His bride, the church, the grime began to be removed from the Masterpiece. I think somehow that Aquila and Priscilla were one of the first couples to see the possibilities for marriage according to God's design. It was their church in Ephesus that received from Paul the instructions to be filled with the Holy Spirit, with the subsequent application to husbands and wives.

How did that impact Aquila and Priscilla? Did it change their relationship and deepen their marriage? There is not a lot of detail about this couple in the New Testament, but reading between the lines leads me to believe that it must have. The story of chapter 16 is speculation but based on facts—they had to escape from Rome under the decree of Claudius. They met Paul in Corinth, and he probably led them to faith in Christ while working alongside them as a tent maker. The couple traveled with Paul to Ephesus, led the great teacher Apollos to faith in Christ, and probably risked their lives to save Paul during the silversmith riots.

Aquila and Priscilla enjoyed an adventure together, one uniquely orchestrated by God to reflect His love for the church. Today God invites every married couple to enjoy that adventure. Of course, not every couple shares the same level of excitement that Aquila and Priscilla did when they met the apostle Paul. That isn't the point. Our adventure together may appear to others as little more than the ordinary daily grind of life. But to us, it is the fabric of meaning.

Jo and I see in Fred and Gwen Landis a painting of exquisite beauty. All their life has been lived in the Pacific Northwest. I would characterize them as faithful to the call God had on them, and that faithfulness has given them a joyful contentment. While they aren't famous, their lives are significant. This couple has perhaps impacted the world just as much or more than Priscilla and Aquila. From their eight small churches have gone perhaps a dozen missionaries, and those missionaries have touched many lives.

That's how the church works. Some marriages have higher visibility; others work behind the scenes. All are significant. This is indeed a mystery, for each couple has the opportunity to reveal some facet of the Masterpiece of Christ and His church.

The Adventure of Marriage

When I think about my life journey with Jo, it feels like a drama and we have just started act three. Act one was the first five years, consisting of our courtship and early years of marriage. Those were fun times of long walks and talks, of deepening faith, of establishing our careers and financial foundation—all highlighted by a nine-week trip across America. Act two opened with the purchase of our first house and the birth of our first child, Joshua. For roughly 25 years we raised and educated our children, started a successful business that lasted six years, moved twice to new cities, and worked toward several financial and career goals. But recently, as our two sons married and our daughter departed for college, the curtain closed on this part of the drama. We are now officially empty nesters!

Jo and I are acutely aware that we are not writing this drama. Or, to return to my original metaphor, our marriage is a picture being painted by the Great Creator. It's not yet complete, but we eagerly await the next brush strokes while admiring the details we can see so far.

Many of the strokes are fun little memories of people Jo and I have hosted in our home. During our first year of marriage, we rented a small one-bedroom apartment in Phoenix. One evening I invited a retired running back from the San Diego Chargers over to consult on my book *One Way to Play Football*. We moved the living room furniture out of the way so he could demonstrate step-by-step the football techniques I had to write about in my book. On another memorable evening, as I served a plate of spaghetti to our guest, the head of a sports ministry, the noodles kept moving as I set the plate down and the whole meal landed in my friend's lap. I was horrified at the time, but our guest was gracious, and that memory provides Jo and me with many a laugh now. (More recently, we had a retired major league pitcher and his wife in our home, and the oven caught on fire as Jo was fixing dinner.)

Before year one ended, we sensed God moving us. As we prayed and talked, it became clear that we should move to Portland, in part to be near my aging parents. While we agreed on this, Jo worried about finding another teaching position, since she wasn't accredited in Oregon. So I went to the local library, got a copy of the Yellow Pages for Portland, and found the addresses of five private schools. Jo wrote to all five, and all five offered her a job! I think that was probably the first realization that our marriage was a joint adventure of faith. There have been many examples since.

Besides adventure, Jo and I share a thirst for knowledge. From the beginning, we have both read many and varied books. We are hungry for good Bible teaching, and we interact about what we hear. But we also learn by understanding that we are joined together by God for our good. While in Portland, I decided to retain an agent to help me with my writing business. Jo agreed that maybe I needed an agent, but she strongly disagreed with the person I chose. It took me a few months and several thousand dollars to learn a very sad lesson, and I ended up firing him. Here was a case where I led and Jo submitted, but I led foolishly, for I didn't listen to the helper God had given me. From that point on, I made no major decisions without fully involving Jo in the process. That didn't make me any less the head of the house, but it certainly did make me wiser.

One thing I've realized about being the head of my wife is that I am responsible for helping her become complete as a person. Today it seems that individual career goals conspire to undermine intimacy in marriage. When two people have supercharged career objectives, sooner or later they are bound to clash. How can we overcome that in our society? Children are one of God's ways to provide a couple with a shared mission.

Jo and I talked about this before we had children and decided she couldn't do justice to her teaching career when children arrived. She felt she needed to stay home and concentrate on their needs.

Six weeks before Joshua's birth, Jo resigned her teaching assign-
ment, and with the exception of a failed one-year experiment, she
stayed home all these years to care for our three children.

At times I asked Jo if she missed teaching—it had been her
career goal since sixth grade. She said that it was an important time
of her life, but it had passed. We often talked and prayed about
what she might do as the children got older and she had more flex-
ibility in her schedule. Jo decided not to go back to a full-time job
but instead looked for alternatives that would allow her always to
be home whenever the kids were home.

It was our friend Gwen Ellis who proposed a solution. For several years I had looked for an author to write a book about interior
decorating that would recognize the budget limitations of many
single-income families. I had discussed this idea with Gwen when
she was managing editor at Focus on the Family, and after she
moved to Michigan to take another publishing job, she suggested,
"Why don't I write that book with Jo? After all, we've both lived
that message."

I thought this was a great idea. Jo wasn't so sure. But with
encouragement from Gwen and me, she gave it a shot. The result
was publication of *Decorating on a Shoestring*, followed shortly by
completion of another manuscript on dressing the family. Suddenly,
Jo was being contacted by publishers, preparing proposals, and discovering that she might actually enjoy writing. As a result, Jo and I
have found another aspect of life we can share together, and I find
I enjoy seeing her succeed as much as or more than my own writing success.

The Great Counselor

Jesus promised to send us a Counselor to be with us forever. The
disciples waited for the outpouring of the Holy Spirit at Pentecost.

The apostle Paul commanded us to be filled with the Holy Spirit. Here I believe is the greatest hope for marriages today. Just as God walked and talked with the first couple in Eden, so God comes to marriages today and offers to be our Counselor, to walk with us and guide us day by day and moment by moment. He doesn't force His way into a marriage. But to those couples who invite His presence, the possibilities are incredible.

This aspect of marriage energizes me. God is in our midst, and when I recognize His presence, I'm in awe. The following experience is one example of how He continues to lead us on a journey of adventure.

Over the years, Jo and I often talked and dreamed about our lives when the nest would be empty, and our hearts were drawn to a certain kind of international missions work. We imagined a joint ministry that might take us a month to three months at a time to various countries to use our gifts with the national church, helping them develop communication strategies to reach their people. And now God is opening that door for us. As I write we are preparing to teach a marriage course to pastors and their wives in a country that is 97 percent Muslim. Next year we are already scheduled to travel and teach in four more countries.

I often think of God's commission to the first couple to fill the earth and rule it and compare it to the commission Jesus left His disciples just before His departure from earth. Jesus said, "Go and make disciples of all nations,...teaching them to obey everything I have commanded you."[1] I wonder if this supersedes God's original commission to Adam and Eve. God calls us not just to sacrifice for each other but together to love the Lord and sacrifice for Him in whatever area of service to which He directs us. Surely this is a charge to capture anyone's imagination. Better yet, this is a challenge for a husband and wife to tackle together.

It was in that context that Jo floated a radical idea on New Year's

196   your
m a r r i a g e
masterpiece

Day in 1998. We were talking in a coffee shop about our plans for the coming year—vacation, how to pay for the children's Christian education, and other major budget items—when out of the blue Jo said, "Would you be open to selling our house and buying something smaller?"

At the time, we were living in our dream home with a view of the Colorado front range. When I asked why she wanted to move, she said one reason was that climbing up and down the stairs of our three-story home hurt her knees, and she was tired of the constant pain. But there was another, more important reason. "We've talked about someday, when the children are grown, being free to work in other countries as God might provide opportunity. Now that the tax laws have changed, we can sell our house, buy a cheaper house, and if we put all the equity into the new house, there is no capital gains tax. We can get a significantly lower mortgage, and if we accelerate payments, we can be completely debt-free in a few years." With a grin she added, "Then we'll be flexible to go wherever God wants us to go and do whatever He wants us to do."

Jo's thinking was brilliant! In that moment, I thought, *I love being married to this woman*. And then I thought, *Thank You, Lord*, for I was sure that this was the Holy Spirit guiding us. I don't think our plan made as much sense to some of our friends, for it was counter to the normal upward-mobility thinking of our society. In fact, there were times as we implemented the plan that we wanted to cling to the bigger house. But a year later, we moved into a smaller ranch-style home that saves wear and tear on Jo's knees. It doesn't have the view I so loved; yet we often comment that we are content. This peace, part of the fruit of the Spirit, is further evidence that God is guiding us.

As I think of these experiences, I believe I can say that Jo and I have, in some mysterious way, returned to Eden. Certainly this world is not paradise. And we are painfully aware of our fallen nature. But when I think back to the first couple and what they had, I can't help but conclude that God has redeemed marriage.

Living the Adventure

While Jo and I were living in Salem, Oregon, we met a fascinating couple, Joe and Kay Kong. I was intrigued when our pastor, Don Bubna at Salem Christian and Missionary Alliance Church, told me about how in 1975 Joe's first wife had died following emergency surgery, leaving him to raise five children alone. After a period of grieving, Joe approached Don and asked, "Pastor, my children need a mother and I need a companion. Will you help me find a wife?"

Arranging marriages is not something most seminaries train pastors to do. But Don knew that Joe's cultural background also had not prepared him to play the dating game. Less than a year before, Joe had arrived from Cambodia, where he was a cabinet minister before the Khmer Rouge overthrew the government. Joe and his family had fled for their lives. Through the church in Salem, Joe had met the Lord Jesus and trusted Him as his Savior. Now Joe was trusting God to provide a wife. Though a new Christian, he confidently reminded Don of the promise of Jesus: "If you remain in me and my words remain in you, ask whatever you wish, and it will be given you."[2]

Meanwhile, thousands of miles away in the Philippines there was a refugee from Laos. Both of her parents had died, and during her teen years her oldest brother had raised her. She had also fled her country because of the war in Southeast Asia and was now working as a broadcaster for Far East Broadcasting Company (FEBC), sending the gospel message back to her homeland.

Through the network of Christian and Missionary Alliance churches, a Cambodian pastor in Southern California contacted Joe and, shortly before Christmas, invited him to spend a weekend at

198   your
m a r r i a g e
masterpiece

his home. That Friday night, the pastor hosted a party. Among the guests were three "candidates"—a Cambodian widow, an American who'd been a missionary teacher in the Philippines, and the Laotian woman who'd arrived in the United States only 23 days earlier. Joe was particularly drawn to the last woman, who spent much of the evening entertaining the children. The two spoke briefly, and the conversation focused on their spiritual journeys.

Late that night, after all the guests had gone home, the pastor and his wife asked Joe which of the three candidates interested him. Without hesitation, Joe named Kay, the young Laotian woman.

The next day, the pastor and his wife took Joe and Kay Christmas shopping, and Joe bought Kay a much-needed winter coat. After attending a Vietnamese church service that night, the four sat in the pastor's living room, and Joe told Kay why he was in Los Angeles. After telling his story, he said, "I believe that God has led me to you. Kay, will you marry me?"

Before leaving Laos, Kay had prayed that God would be her Father. Since no earthly father could arrange her marriage, she prayed that God would be the arranger. She determined that she would recognize God's choice for her if the man loved God first and foremost, came to where she lived, and proposed marriage in front of two or more people.

So here was Joe Kong, who loved God more than anything in life, visited her in Southern California, and proposed marriage in front of the pastor and his wife. *But, Lord, he has five children!* she protested in silent prayer. That hadn't been part of her request.

While silently waiting on God for a couple of minutes, she seemed to sense Him saying, "Will you minister to those five children?"

Kay looked up and said to Joe, "Yes, I will marry you." For the next hour, the two couples thanked God for His provision and prayed that the Holy Spirit would put the fire of love and passion in Joe's and Kay's hearts. After attending church the next morning, Joe flew home to Salem.

There was a crisis a few days later when Kay called Joe. Crying, she told him her friends were telling her she was crazy to do this and urging her to change her mind. Many warned her about the dangers of being a stepmother, saying that the children who come to the States from foreign cultures rebel against the old ways and cause no end of problems.

Joe gently urged his fiancée to stop crying and keep praying. "If this is God's will, no one can separate us. If it's not His will, then neither of us want it." Joe then wrote a 10-page testimony for Kay to give to her friends. He also went to Don Bubna and the church elders and sought their blessing. The church board voted unanimously to support Joe. And so the couple was married on April 23, and to add to the blessing, Dr. Berthemen, executive director for FEBC, made all the arrangements and paid for the wedding.

This is not a "happily ever after" story. While Kay had spent hours talking with the children by phone every Saturday morning, they did not meet until after the wedding. To go from being a single woman to mother of five children is not easy, but Joe believed "we have the very best Counselor in the Holy Spirit to guide us." There were a lot of complaints from the kids as Kay brought some much-needed order to the family. For example, the children were used to rising and eating breakfast in front of the television. Kay insisted they get dressed first, then eat at the table. Of course, the children ran to Joe to complain when he got home from work. But Joe always deferred to his wife. Whatever she said was final.

It took a year to establish a routine in the home. A kind woman from church helped by taking Kay shopping and teaching her the ways of a strange culture. She also taught her how to can and freeze food to take advantage of the area's fresh produce. There were tough times as the elder children went through the teenage years and

200   your
m a r r i a g e
masterpiece

struggled with the clash of cultures. Then four years after they were married, Kay became pregnant and Timmy was born. The new addition seemed to bring the family closer together.

Besides their shared faith and their children, one thing that has cemented this couple is their joy of serving God together. As their children grew, more opportunities opened. Kay continued to make recordings for FEBC to beam to Laos from the Philippines. She was also trained in Bible translation, and after 10 years she completed a translation of the Old Testament into Laotian. Joe worked with Cambodian churches in the Pacific Northwest, helping to plant five new congregations. In 1986, Joe was elected district superintendent over all the U.S. Cambodian congregations in the Christian and Missionary Alliance. The election meant moving the family to Southern California, where many of the churches were located. Joe served four three-year terms before being asked to head up inter-cultural ministries for the denomination. His work gives him over-sight of 530 ethnic congregations—about 28 percent of the denomination—around the United States.

Jo and I have reunited with this dear couple now that we both live in Colorado Springs. Their children are grown—the youngest, Timmy, is in his twenties. Six grandchildren have been added to the family.

The couple remains in awe of how God has orchestrated their lives together. Joe says, "I wouldn't be in ministry today if all this hadn't happened. God worked it all out for good. I feel like Abraham must have felt when he trusted God and left his home to go to a new land. Ours is not a culture story; it is God's story."

The couple celebrated their 30th wedding anniversary in April 2007, and Kay says, "We have fallen more and more in love over the years. We look back and realize that we are just little people. God called us and we were willing to listen, and look at all that He has done!"

Look at all God has done! That is the theme of the Kongs' marriage, and it should be what we see in every marriage. But many find it impossible to see beyond the trials in their relationship to the wonderful picture God is creating. Jo and I, like many couples, are blessed with a happy marriage; remaining faithful through "better and worse" has paid off. But for many, the payoff hasn't arrived, and they despair, wondering if it's worth the effort.

So a nagging question remains. I realize that marriage is not about my happiness but about self-sacrifice for the glory of God. I have seen that marriage as God intended in Eden can be had today. But in our fallen world, that doesn't always bring happiness. The question that our culture asks is this: "Where's the payoff?" Why should I be heroic in my marriage?

To answer that question, I need to examine one more detail of God's marriage, an event that has yet to occur but that provides the payoff for persevering through the good times and the bad times of marriage.

18

Michael Proposes a Toast

There is a payoff for faithfully going the distance in marriage. One day, there will be a celebration like none we have ever seen. At that time, we will finally see the picture God has been painting in our lives and marriages. It's almost impossible to imagine what that experience will be like. But it's worth trying, because it is so motivational. So for our final vignette, let's look one more time through the eyes of the two angels Abdiel and Zephon.

There had never been such a party in heaven. It started with a fanfare of trumpets. Then a glorious voice from the throne of God said, "Praise our God, all you His servants!"

That was the cue for the angelic choir to shout. Abdiel had looked forward to this moment. As part of the great multitude of heaven, he put his whole being into the words "Hallelujah! For our Lord God Almighty reigns. Let us rejoice and be glad and give Him glory! For the wedding of the Lamb has come, and His bride has made herself ready." The sound was incredible, like the roar of rushing rapids in a great river and like loud explosions of thunder.

"Fine linen, bright and clean, was given her to wear." With those words, all of heaven gazed at the bride slowly approaching her husband. Her face beamed with joy greater than any bride on earth had ever known. Her gown was composed of all her righteous deeds throughout history. It was a sight that mere words could not capture, and Abdiel and all the angels were stunned at the incredible beauty they now observed.

The bride seemed oblivious to the heavenly host that surrounded her. Her eyes gazed on the One who loved her, and all the angels turned with her to view the All-Powerful One, their Master, the Creator, the One who loved His creatures and paid the greatest price for His love. All of history had waited for this moment.

There was a great trumpet blast, and the voice of an angel announced: "Blessed are those who are invited to the wedding supper of the Lamb!"

The angels now observed their Lord in His glory as He sat on a white horse. This was the moment they had longed for, to see Him in power and glory and united with His beloved. One writer tried to describe the Bridegroom: "His eyes are like blazing fire, and on His head are many crowns. He has a name written on Him that no one knows but He Himself. He is dressed in a robe dipped in blood, and His name is the Word of God."

Following the King was the army of heaven. Though he knew many in this army, Abdiel wasn't part of this great host, riding on white horses and dressed in fine linen. Abdiel had other responsibilities, and he hurried now to assume his post for the great feast. He would be serving at the tables.

The angels certainly knew how to throw a party. They had celebrated the day each one of these guests had repented and sought their Lord in humility. But this time, rather than revelers, the angels were servants, which gave them great joy. Reclining at long tables in the banquet hall, the chosen were feted with the finest in food, with flavors rarely if ever achieved on earth. Abdiel was busy clearing dishes and replacing them with the next course, then filling the goblets with the finest of wine. This work was an absolute joy for the angel, for his Master was celebrating His marriage. This was the day they'd all anticipated.

Many courses had already concluded when a voice like a trumpet rang through the banquet hall. "May I have your attention, please!" Everyone immediately stopped eating and turned their attention to the head table. There a most majestic creature stood and held up a magnificent cup of gold covered with sparkling diamonds, rubies, and other gems.

"For those of you who might not know me, allow me to introduce myself. I am the archangel Michael!"

The audience laughed and applauded enthusiastically.

"And I would like to propose a toast!"

Abdiel backed away from the table and glanced along the wall. His friend Zephon was standing there, just a little ways down. Abdiel quickly went and stood beside him.

"Today, we celebrate a marriage. This is the wedding feast we have all anticipated since the great days of Creation millennia ago."

A great cheer erupted, and Michael patiently waited for the noise to subside. When calm returned, Michael continued, "In the Scriptures, in the epistle known as Hebrews, there is a list of the great heroes of faith. We all know their names: Abel, Enoch, Noah, Abraham, Isaac, Jacob, Joseph, Moses, and many more, both named and unnamed. All were commended for their faith, yet none of them received what had been promised. But today, the Scriptures are fulfilled. Today, all receive what was promised!"

An even greater cheer erupted, and the guests stood and applauded and yelled, "Hallelujah! Salvation and glory and power

belong to our God!" Abdiel and Zephon joined all the angels that
surrounded the tables in the great shout of praise to the Lord.
Michael was shouting with them. He was in no hurry to continue
his speech, for there was no time limit. Indeed, time was meaningless now.

All were laughing with joy as they again reclined and Michael
began the next phase of his toast. "I would now like to celebrate the
great masterpiece of our Lord, the picture He created on earth to
give us in heaven a glimpse of this great day we now celebrate.
From the moment he created the first man and first woman and
joined them in marriage, it was His desire that through this union
of man and woman all creation would gain a little understanding of
our Lord's unfathomable love for mankind. Every marriage on earth
was intended to be a foretaste of this great day. Some of those marriages were gems that reflected facets of the incredible love of the
Lamb and His bride. You might say they were some of the frescoes
that all together make up the Great Masterpiece. I would like to recognize some of those masterpiece marriages.

"I begin with Benjamin and Naomi. Their fathers arranged this
marriage when Benjamin was 17 and Naomi was only 14 years old.
They never even met before their wedding day. They were scared,
yet they trusted that their parents had made a good choice. Benjamin worked hard as a stonemason to provide for his family, which
soon contained five children. Two of those children died from illness. Benjamin and Naomi wept and prayed, wondering why God
would allow two little ones to be taken away. There was another
tragedy when a flood wiped out their home and they had to start all
over again. They clung to each other for comfort and were amazed
at how love emerged over the years.

"I salute this marriage because of its ironclad commitment.
This couple never wavered, though at first they didn't have any feelings for each other. Further, Benjamin and Naomi were totally com-

mitted to their faith in our Lord, and as they constantly went to Him for comfort, they drew closer together as a couple. They believed that our Lord really does work all things for good. Would you both come forward now and receive your reward!"

The room exploded in cheers as Benjamin and Naomi made their way to the throne, their faces beaming with joy. As they reached the throne, words were spoken to them. Abdiel couldn't hear what was said, but obviously the couple were thrilled at what they heard.

As Michael began to toast another couple, Abdiel turned to Zephon and suggested, "Let's go a little closer and see if we can hear what our Lord says to the next couple." They moved down the wall toward the front to get a better vantage point.

"The next couple I wish to recognize are Robert and Frances. This couple fell madly in love with each other the day they first met as teenagers, and no one could keep them away from each other. Robert always brought Frances flowers when he visited. Frances used her talents as a chef to fix the finest gourmet meals. Robert would always work beside her to clean the dishes, then bring out his guitar to play and sing for her late into the night. They promised their love to each other and couldn't wait for their wedding day.

"But those were perilous times, and war was declared. Robert was called into service and had to report for duty before they were married. They were separated for the next four years, but they wrote hundreds of letters to each other. Robert had many opportunities to fulfill his longings with strange women in a strange land. But he had promised himself to one, and where some of his buddies failed, Robert refused to have any woman but Frances.

"Robert and Frances finally were married, and their union lasted 44 years. They never stopped showing each other their love. They always held hands on their walks. Robert would bring Frances flowers nearly every day from their garden. And every night as they knelt by their bed in prayer, they each thanked our Lord for giving the other to love. This couple daily recognized their love for each other as a reflection of God's love for them, and they never lost that sense of awe that God had brought them together."

Michael lifted his cup and announced, "To Robert and Frances!" The room erupted in applause. "Please come forward!" Michael shouted to the couple. The two made their way forward, holding hands and beaming at their Lord seated on the throne.

Abdiel leaned forward and heard the Lord speak, "Well done, good and faithful servants." But he couldn't make out the rest of the words.

Michael then announced that he wanted next to recognize "the world's most opposite couple." Immediately several couples responded nearly in unison, "You must mean us!" and everyone in the room laughed.

Michael joined in the hilarity, then continued, "Well, Chuck and Barb *claimed* they were the world's most incompatible couple. Here are a few examples: Barb was left-handed; Chuck was right-handed. Barb was a low-energy person; Chuck was high-energy. Barb liked her applesauce hot; Chuck liked ice crystals in his applesauce. Barb liked her honey thin; Chuck wanted his just on the verge of turning to sugar. Barb was relationship-oriented; Chuck was goal-oriented. Barb was practical; Chuck was a dreamer. Barb liked soft background music; Chuck liked his music loud. Barb was a perfectionist; Chuck was disorderly.

"Well, I can't tell you all of their differences or we'd be here nearly forever! It's ironic that before they were married they believed they were perfectly compatible. Those differences only emerged after their wedding day. By their count, they documented well over 500 distinct differences, and I might add, our Master tells me there were many more they didn't recognize. Those differences did cause a lot of conflict, but Chuck and Barb were committed to working through those issues, and many times they actually appreciated those differences. Representing all the 'incompatible' couples, Chuck and Barb please come forward."

As the Lord complimented this couple, the banquet room buzzed with excited couples remembering and laughing about their own unique differences, so Abdiel was still unable to hear what the Lord said to the couple.

"I would now like to recognize a remarkable woman," Michael announced. "Janet did not have a happy marriage. She married a man who said he loved our Lord, but his heart deceived him. Janet endured years of abuse, verbal and even occasionally physical. She cared for their two children, and through her love she honored her husband as the head of their home. Many a night she would pray, *Lord, this is for You*, as she fixed him a late meal or carried out one of his orders. After 15 years, Janet's husband left her for a younger woman. She wept and prayed but let him go."

There was a dramatic pause, and everyone in heaven eagerly waited for the punch line. "Janet, today you receive your reward. Our Lord saw every one of your tears and heard every one of your prayers. He accepted all the love you gave your husband as His. Would you please come forward now!"

Janet practically ran into the arms of her Beloved, weeping tears of joy. Gently, those tears were wiped away. "Well done, good and faithful servant. There will be no more death or mourning or crying or pain, for the old order of things has passed away." And all in the banquet hall shouted and then burst into an anthem of praise to the Lamb, while Janet stayed in the arms of her Beloved, and no one said she had to leave.

"This next couple demonstrated heroic stamina in their marriage," Michael announced. "I'm speaking of Ivan and Carolyn. Shortly after they were married, Ivan was injured in a war and was bedridden for nearly a year. Carolyn moved to the army hospital and spent every day caring for him. Every night, before leaving his side, Carolyn prayed for her husband. Ivan lost a leg because of an infection, and the doctors weren't able to remove all of the shrapnel from his body. But this couple was unwavering in their dedication to each other.

"Later in their lives, after the birth of their second child, Carolyn suffered a debilitating depression. Ivan hobbled around the farm, doing his chores, and cared for the children as best he could. He never raised a word in anger to his wife, though he was frustrated that she often was unable even to get out of bed. Each night, before going to sleep, he knelt by her bed and prayed for his wife. It was more than a year before she was able to resume her household responsibilities.

"This couple demonstrated heroic love to each other through difficult situations and never even considered escaping their situation. Ivan and Carolyn, please come forward." The joyful couple, with Ivan now skipping on his healthy legs, practically ran to the throne where Abdiel heard the Lord say, "Well done, good and faithful servants. Enter into the joy of the Lord!"

"Did you hear that?" Abdiel asked Zephon.

"Yes, this is the reward promised in the Scriptures. In our Lord's parable of the talents, these were the words spoken to the faithful servants who increased the talents given to them."

"What do you think the joy of the Lord is?"

"Quiet! Michael speaks again."

"The next couple I want to recognize lived a rather exciting life, to say the least! They set the pattern for many marriages in the centuries that followed. You might say they were glued together by adventure, and by our wonderful Lord through His Holy Spirit. Let's recount a few of their adventures:

"As a young couple, having been married only a couple of years, they had to escape from Rome because of the decree of the emperor Claudius. They settled in Corinth, where they took an itinerant preacher into their home and business and listened as this preacher opened the Scriptures and revealed to them the wonderful news of Jesus the Christ. They were baptized and became leaders in the young congregation. When the preacher decided to move on to other mission fields, this couple went with him and settled in Ephesus. There they heard another gifted preacher, who preached the baptism of John. They invited him to dinner and told him the rest of the story!"

By now the crowd recognized who this couple was and roared its appreciation. Michael continued: "A couple of years later, during the riot of the silversmiths, this couple risked their lives to pull Paul out of danger. Eventually, they returned to Rome, where this story began, and there they used their home for one of the churches in the city. I speak, of course, of the tent-maker couple Aquila and Priscilla, whom Paul called 'my fellow workers in Christ Jesus. They risked their lives for me. Not only I but all the churches of the Gentiles are grateful to them.' Would you please come forward!"

There were many more celebrations of masterpiece marriages. Abdiel was enthralled by their stories, and with each couple who were recognized, he shouted for joy to the Creator. He also noted the intimacy between the One on the Throne and each couple, a closeness that none of the angels could ever experience. Marriage was foreign to these great beings.

Abdiel continued to wonder about the meaning of the words "Enter into the joy of your Lord."

Zephon was also mulling these words as he said, "You know how the Creator said at the first marriage that the man and woman shall become one flesh."

"Yes," Abdiel responded. "And remember how Jesus prayed at the end of His life that He and His disciples would be one, just as He and His Father are one."

"Two become one in marriage. Today we celebrate the marriage of the Lamb and the church. The two become one."

"But how do the two unite? We know that, on earth, husband and wife joined together physically and that their union was often the cause of great ecstasy. But here, in this marriage…" He couldn't complete the thought.

Zephon laughed. "No, I don't think it's the same. But the physical union of a man and a wife was symbolic of the union God desired with humans. But how that union is achieved, I don't know."

"You don't think the words 'Enter into the joy of the Lord!' mean they are… No, it can't mean that!"

"I think it's time to serve another course," Zephon interrupted. "We must get back to our tasks."

19

Living Out the
Masterpiece

There is a great celebration coming—a divine wedding feast! Then we will see the complete picture of marriage that God is creating and understand the part our individual marriages have within His Masterpiece.

This truth helps me realize that our desire for a fulfilling marriage can be met. God offers us meaning in marriage first by showing us His marriage; second, by inviting us to follow His model, offering us the Holy Spirit as our Counselor; and finally, by assuring us that those who faithfully follow this plan will receive God's approval: "Well done, good and faithful servant."

This wonderful news removes the grime of disappointment or regret we all feel to some degree, at certain times, in our marriages. No doubt there are some readers who are on their second or third marriages. They can't go back and change the past. The mistakes have been made. What God presents to us is the opportunity to let Him do a good work in our marriage starting today. Regardless of your past, there is a beautiful picture He wants to create in your life and marriage.

As I was finishing this book, a friend of mine wrote, "There is no such thing as an insignificant little marriage." He's absolutely right! Every marriage provides a unique opportunity for God to reveal Himself to the people around that couple. And perhaps the audience for this drama is greater than we imagine: A marriage as God intended may be one of the greatest declarations of His character to all the heavenly hosts.

Choosing Right in the Small Things

Ravi Zacharias has written, "A fulfilled life is one that has the will of God as its focus, not the appetite of the flesh."[1] There is the great contrast. And the great choice.

A few years ago, I was sorting through my mail, which included a monthly club offer to purchase music. Among the enticements were some inexpensive boxed sets. They would provide a great way to expand my library. As I considered the offer, I read these words: "Indulge yourself!"

That is the message being shouted at us a thousand different ways every day. You deserve this. Give yourself a break. Make yourself happy. That thinking has permeated our culture's thinking about marriage. If I'm not careful, it's easy to believe that I'm free to do anything I want. Except I am married, and my marriage is about more than me and my momentary happiness. For Jo and me, our marriage is a covenant relationship that God wants to use for His glory to give the world a glimpse of what He is like.

As I look at the ad for music, do I respond any differently because I'm married? Society would say no. And certainly, this doesn't seem like a big issue. But I belong to my wife, and she is one with me. If I think only of myself, I'm acting selfishly. Those words "indulge yourself" jarred me and actually caused me to start thinking differently about the offer. I knew that this month our family faced a number of extra expenditures. One car needed servicing before our son Jonathan used it in driving school. Our older son was graduating and there would be extra expenses associated with that event. Further, Anna's shoes were too small, and it was time to pay reenrollment fees for school. In that context, my little decision suddenly wasn't so insignificant. At the least, I should discuss it with my wife. Or I could simply refuse the offer, knowing there would probably be another opportunity in a month or two.

Refusing a music offer may seem like a small thing, but self-sacrifice is about doing small things for the good of the marriage.

Looking in the Wrong Places

I think this was where Jim, the baseball player, struggled. The last time I saw Jim was a few months after our talk in the Diablo Stadium parking lot. I was in Seattle on business. It happened that Jim's team was playing a series in Tacoma, just a 45-minute drive south. I called him late that morning and arranged to meet him at his hotel room.

I arrived about two p.m., two hours before he had to leave for the ballpark. Jim and his roommate were typical ballplayers, with suitcases lying open and clothes strewn around the room. In two days they would have to pack up and move on to the next city for another series of games. Jim welcomed me warmly. Ignoring the soap opera his roommate was watching on television, we talked about his season. He was pitching long relief. He'd had a few good outings but also some times when he'd been roughed up. Consistency remained his problem. He already knew he would not make it to the major leagues that season.

"So, are you thinking you'll retire from baseball?" I asked.

"No way!" Jim replied. "If I'm released, I'll get picked up by another club. I know I can still pitch in the big leagues. I can't give up now." I knew Jim wasn't facing reality. There were younger prospects ready for promotion. No team was going to want an inconsistent and aging pitcher.

As we talked, I noticed a stack of *Playboy* magazines lying by his bed. Jim noticed my eye going there and said, "They help pass the time when we're on the road."

"How are things with Bonnie?" I asked, ignoring the pornography.

"Okay right now. I think we actually do better during the season when we're apart half the time."

"Does she still want you to quit ball?"

"She hasn't said anything about it since the season started. But silence isn't golden." He laughed and said, "We both know we have to face our differences sooner or later." Then he turned serious and said, "I don't know, Al. She's a good person, and I don't want to hurt her. But I don't have any feelings for her anymore. I suppose we were in love once, but I don't feel it now."

I couldn't help but wonder where those feelings had gone. Did it have anything to do with the pictures in the magazines beside his bed? I wondered, was Jim in love with Bonnie, the person, or was he in love with the image of Bonnie, the way she used to be? I'd seen Bonnie and Jim's wedding pictures, so I knew she had gained 15 or 20 pounds since then. More seriously, I wondered if all Jim really wanted was a trophy wife who would make him look good, not someone who challenged him to be a responsible husband. If so, no wonder Jim wasn't satisfied. The pictures in the magazines no doubt led to fantasies of adoring women who thought he could do no wrong and provided him endless pleasure. When he returned home, he was reminded that reality was a very different picture.

What struck me was how hard Jim pursued happiness, and how elusive it seemed. In contrast, I thought of the words of Christ: "Whoever finds his life will lose it, and whoever loses his life for my sake will find it."[2] Jim was looking in the wrong places for life.

Where the Rubber Meets the Road

The battle for happiness rages in marriage. Our choice is between God's way and the alternatives presented by the world. Let's face it, there are so many attractive people around us, at our workplace, on our business travels, even at church—people who are interesting and who might fill gaps we think we perceive in our lives. There are seductive images from Madison Avenue, and now on the Internet, that barge into our lives uninvited. And behind all these temptations lies an enemy who bides his time, looking for any weakness by which to destroy a marriage. Just as he set a trap for Adam and Eve in Eden, far too often today one of his traps suddenly snaps shut and claims yet another victim.

I know that women as well as men face temptations. My wife has told me of occasions when men indicated an interest in her. Thankfully, she hasn't allowed them any encouragement. What keeps Jo and me from straying off course in our exclusivity? It is our participating in something much greater than us. This wonderful truth is a great help to us: *We are married to Christ!* We are part of the church, and the church is the bride of Christ. Therefore, He and Jo and I—the three of us—are married. This is the truth that every Christian couple can experience. Of course, all believers in Christ can experience marriage on a divine level regardless of whether or not they have a good marriage on earth, or even marry at all as human beings.

Winning the Battle

The apostle Paul urges us, "Do not conform any longer to the pattern of this world, but be transformed by the renewing of your
mind."[3] The only way to render mute the messages of society is to
overwhelm them with the truths of Scripture. I have found that one
way to do that is to meet regularly with a group of like-minded
believers.

For a couple of years I was involved with a men's group where
we frequently talked about the issues of marital fidelity and dealing
with temptation. Everyone in the group said they faced similar
struggles, including an older man named Otto. He, however, also
offered some helpful encouragement. "One of the best ways I've
learned to combat my mental battles is simply to concentrate on
loving my wife."

"What do you mean?" I asked.

"Here's an example. Every time you see a woman, or an image
comes into your mind, immediately pray, *God, I thank You for my
wife. Please teach me how to love her just as Christ loved the church.*
(I've prayed that prayer many times—often many times in the same
day.) Then act on that love. Think about something you can do for
your wife. Maybe you give her a call from your office to tell her you
love her. Or plan to take her on a coffee date after dinner. Or write
her a little love note and leave it someplace where she will find it
during the day."

"I can do those things," I said.

"Here's the thing," Otto continued. "When you continually do
these little things, you know you are reflecting God's heart. Even if
you don't feel love at the time you're doing them, do them anyway.
It's dangerous to rely on your feelings. Many times I do things for
my wife not because I feel like it but because it's right. Then, over
time, the feelings of love emerge."

Tears welled up in Otto's eyes as he spoke. Haltingly, he said, "Men, today I feel more love for my wife than I could ever have imagined on our wedding day." Recently, Otto celebrated his 40th wedding anniversary.

Transcendent Moments

I still often think of Jim and Bonnie and what they lost by not finishing the marriage they started. The sad thing is that they probably don't know what they lost. If only Jim had followed Otto's wisdom and done what was right despite his feelings. Society is so obsessed with the search for self-fulfillment that when someone isn't happy in a marriage, it's hard to persevere in the face of attractive alternatives. So the tendency is to look outward for that perfect person who will give "real" happiness.

My journey with Jo and my study of the Grand Romance, the Masterpiece, has convinced me that far more is gained by staying married and allowing God to finish the painting He is creating in my marriage. While some feel trapped by such a commitment, I have found that within our covenant marriage there is almost always contentment, often genuine happiness, and occasionally breathtaking moments of pure joy.

An epiphany came one magical night on the central Oregon coast. Jo and I had taken our children to a friend's two-bedroom condominium just north of Waldport for a week of rest and relaxation. I love this particular spot because there is no telephone that can interrupt me, and the rugged beach opens up for a couple of miles in each direction. On weekdays there is rarely a person to be seen. That week we watched squalls roll in off the ocean, lash our apartment, and move on into the coastal mountains. Between showers we walked on the beach and looked for shells and unusual pieces of driftwood. Joshua flew his kite in the stiff breeze while

220   your
m a r r i a g e
masterpiece

Jonathan built a major highway system in the sand, eagerly assisted by his little sister, who had only recently started toddling.

On Saturday, I had to speak at a conference in Eugene. That morning there were no clouds over the ocean, only glorious blue sky. I enjoyed a two-hour drive, spoke a couple of times, then drove back to Waldport in late afternoon. This was one of those rare days on the Oregon coast when temperatures soared into the 70s and one could actually wear short sleeves and shorts. Jo prepared a magnificent dinner, after which we walked out onto the beach and began strolling along the surf. Jo, Joshua, and Anna removed their shoes and walked along the waterline. Anna squealed with excitement every time the water got close, dashing away to escape its fingers until a tidal surge tickled her toes and she laughed for joy. Jonathan wasn't comfortable around the water and preferred to keep his distance, skipping near me in the sand like a little colt.

On that glorious evening, it suddenly hit me. Watching my wife and three children, soaking up the evening sun, listening to the rhythmic roar of the ocean, I experienced the most intense feeling of contentment and joy. I was so surprised that I had to stop walking for a moment to absorb the emotion. At that instant, I realized there was *nothing* in this world that could make me any happier. It wouldn't have mattered if I was a pauper or the richest person in the world. My happiness had nothing to do with what I had or hadn't achieved.

I had to ask myself why I was so happy. Why was I so utterly fulfilled that I don't believe I could have felt any more happiness? The answer was very simple. I was enjoying one of the most glorious spots in God's creation with the woman I loved dearly and three children that were the fruit of our union, and all of this was happening in the presence of God, who felt so near that I could almost touch Him. For a while, time seemed to stop, and as I looked at Jo, I knew she was feeling it as well. When the sun touched the horizon, we returned to the condominium and put the children to bed. Then Jo and I sat next to each other, gazed through the picture window at the afterglow of a glorious sunset, and savored a transcendent moment that we wished would never end.

I believe that evening I experienced a hint of the unending joy we will know in heaven. I have longed for more of those moments, but they seem maddeningly elusive, at least from my experience and that of my friends. They certainly can't be programmed but seem to emerge when least expected. It's as though God serves us just a thimbleful at a time to encourage us to keep going in the grind of daily life.

But having tasted this once, my senses are alert to other moments in my marriage when I might gain a glimpse of the glory to come. When we experience those moments, Jo and I savor them, and a sense of gratitude wells up within us. We speak our thankfulness to God for bringing us together, realizing that He is central to our marriage. And we express our excitement about seeing where He will take us next on our journey together, leading to that final celebration when we, as part of the church, are united to our Beloved forever.

With Gratitude

The message for this book began to crystallize on a dry-erase board in Kurt Bruner's office. Kurt was vice president over the Focus Resource Group and my boss at Focus on the Family. We were brainstorming what message our organization should develop that might add a fresh perspective to the many books already published on marriage. We began looking together at the Scriptures, and many of the concepts you've just read emerged in that session. Kurt, thank you for allowing me to write this book. This is as much your message as it is mine.

Several members of the Focus on the Family book development team played major roles in this project. They include Larry Weeden, managing editor, who guided me through the early drafts of the manuscript; Mick Silva, who also read early drafts and helped to write the study guide; and Ray Seldomridge, who did the final editing of the manuscript.

There were many who reviewed the manuscript in various stages and provided valuable input. I particularly wish to thank Jim Ware, Steve and Lisa Halliday, Kent Hill, Dave Tillstrom, and Craig and Kat Osten for their advice and encouragement.

Thanks also to members of our international team who reviewed the manuscript, including Bruce Peppin, Jonathan Booth, Jef De Vriese, Wee Min Lee, Tim Cole, and Win Morgan.

Our brand management team has worked many hours on the strategy, packaging, and promotion of the book. Many thanks to Julie Kuss, Stacey Herebic, Edie Hutchinson, and Clark Miller, as well as the marketing and sales team at Tyndale House.

A special thanks to my assistant, Kim Atkins, for finding books, typing notes, making phone calls, running copies, condensing the manuscript for the audio book, and covering for me during the many days when I was hiding away in order to finish writing.

And most important, a special thank-you to my wife, Jo. She read every word of this manuscript in various drafts and provided a listening ear as I talked through the content. Jo, the message of this book is *our* message. It's a joy making this journey with you!

Notes

Prologue

1. Information about Sistine Chapel gleaned from *The Sistine Chapel: A Glorious Restoration* by Fabrizio Mancinelli and Carlo Pietrangeli, Harry N. Abrams, Inc., 1994; *An Unfamiliar Michelangelo* by Robert Hughes, *Time*, Feb. 11, 1985, pg. 82; *Out of Grime, a Domain of Light* by Robert Hughes, *Time*, April 27, 1987, pg. 86; *High Tech and Old Masters* by William D. Marbach, *Newsweek*, March 30, 1987, pg. 70; and *He Didn't Paint by the Numbers, but He's Digitized Now; Michelangelo* by Gina Maranto, *Discover*, May 1987, pg. 8.

2. According to a United Nations survey. See "Survey: 9 of 10 Still Say 'I Do'" by Joan Lowy, Scripps-Howard News Service, June 29, 2000.

Chapter 1

1. Jim and Bonnie are pseudonyms. Details have been changed about their story to protect their identity. Throughout the book, where a name is marked by an "*", it means the names and other identifying characteristics have been changed.

2. See *The State of Our Unions 2000: The Social Health of Marriage in America*. Regarding the divorce rate, the report states that it is slightly less than it was in the early 1980s. "In view of the lowering of divorce rates in the last few decades, the statement '50 percent of all marriages will end in divorce' may no longer be accurate. If the divorce rates of the late 1990s were to persist into the future, not much more than

40 percent of today's first marriages would end in divorce, and less than 50 percent of all marriages would end in either divorce or permanent separation" (pg. 17).

3. *Flying Solo* by Tamala M. Edwards, *Time*, August 28, 2000.
4. "Divorce for the Best" by Philip D. Harvey, *Washington Post*, July 11, 2000, pg. A23.
5. "Are Traditional Marriages a Thing of the Past?" by Cheryl K. Chumley, CNS News, August 9, 2000.

Chapter 2

1. Genesis 1:27.
2. This work of speculation and imagination is based on Job 38:4-7, where God speaks to Job and says, "Where were you when I laid the earth's foundation? Tell me, if you understand. Who marked off its dimensions? Surely you know! Who stretched a measuring line across it? On what were its footings set, or who laid its cornerstone—while the morning stars sang together *and all the angels shouted for joy*?" (emphasis added). Apparently God had quite an appreciative audience for His work of Creation! Other scriptures that imply that angels observe the drama taking place on earth include 1 Timothy 5:21, Hebrews 12:22, and 1 Peter 1:12.

Chapter 3

1. Genesis 1:28.
2. Genesis 1:29.
3. Genesis 2:25.
4. Genesis 1:27.
5. Genesis 3:8.
6. Genesis 1:28.
7. Genesis 1:27.
8. Genesis 2:24.

9. "Sex and the Single Christian," an interview with Steve Tracy, *ChristianityToday*.com, posted July 7, 2000.
10. Mason, Mike, *The Mystery of Marriage*, 1985, Multnomah Press, pg. 30.
11. Ibid., pp. 58-59.

Chapter 4

1. See Genesis 3:6. When Eve took some of the fruit and ate it, "she also gave some to her husband, who was with her, and he ate it."

Chapter 5

1. See 1 Timothy 2:14.
2. St. Augustine, *The City of God*, Doubleday Image Book edition, 1958, page 307.
3. See Ephesians 1:3-14.
4. Genesis 2:17.
5. Waite, Linda J., and Gallagher, Maggie, *The Case for Marriage*, New York, 2000, Doubleday, pg. 148.
6. Ibid.
7. Wallerstein, Judith S., Lewis, Julia A., and Blakeslee, Sandra, *The Unexpected Legacy of Divorce*, 2000, Hyperion, pg. 295.
8. Ibid., pg. 304.
9. Gabler, Neal, *Life the Movie: How Entertainment Conquered Reality*, 2000, Vintage Books, pg. 176.
10. Isaiah 54:5.
11. Jeremiah 31:32.
12. Ezekiel 16:8.

Chapter 6

1. The incidents in this story are based on Genesis 12:1-7, 13:14-17, and 15:1-21.

Chapter 7

1. Vander Laan, Ray, with Judith Markham, *Echoes of His Presence*, 1996, Focus on the Family, pp. 6-7.
2. See Revelation 19:9.
3. "If...no proof of the girl's virginity can be found, she shall be brought to the door of her father's house and there the men of her town shall stone her to death" (Deuteronomy 22:20-21).

    "If a man happens to meet in a town a virgin pledged to be married and he sleeps with her, you shall take both of them to the gate of that town and stone them to death—the girl because she was in a town and did not scream for help, and the man because he violated another man's wife" (Deuteronomy 22:23-24).
4. See Matthew 1:18-21 and Luke 1:26-38.
5. "Ka-ching! Wedding price tag nears $30K." Viewed at CNNMoney.com. Go to http://money.cnn.com/2005/05/20/pf/weddings/ Last viewed October 11, 2007.
6. Genesis 12:1.
7. Wallerstein, Judith S., Lewis, Julia A., and Blakeslee, Sandra, *The Unexpected Legacy of Divorce*, 2000, Hyperion, pp. 31, 33, 34 (italics in original text).
8. Waite, Linda J., and Gallagher, Maggie, *The Case for Marriage*, 2000, Doubleday, pg. 46.
9. See Genesis 17:9-14.
10. *Book of Common Prayer*, London, Oxford University Press (no copyright date), pg. 312 (emphasis added).
11. Ibid.
12. Ibid., pg. 315.
13. Compiled and edited by Wheeler, Joe L., *Heart to Heart: Stories of Love*, 2000, a Focus on the Family book published

by Tyndale House, pp. 153-158. "Johnny Lingo's Eight-Cow Wife" by Patricia McGerr was originally published in *Woman's Day* in November 1965 and condensed in the February 1966 *Reader's Digest*.

14. Sioban Roberts, National Post, 12/30/00, taken from Smart Marriages Web site. See www.smartmarriages.com.
15. Mark 10:9.
16. Deuteronomy 23:23.

Chapter 9

1. The story was reconstructed with inspiration from J. Vernon McGee, *Through the Bible*, vol. 3, 1982, Thomas Nelson, pp. 142-147.
2. Hosea 2:14.
3. Jeremiah 2:2.
4. Hosea 11:8.
5. Isaiah 49:15-16.
6. Isaiah 54:10.
7. Jeremiah 31:3.
8. Zephaniah 3:17.
9. Job 19:27.
10. Psalm 42:1-2.
11. Psalm 61:4.
12. Psalm 63:1.
13. Psalm 84:1-2.
14. *NIV Bible Commentary (abridgment), volume 1: Old Testament,* Kenneth L. Barker and John Kohlenberger III, consulting editors, 1994, Zondervan, pg. 1027.
15. See Matthew 5:27-28.
16. Ecclesiastes 2:1-2, 8b, 10-11.
17. 1 Corinthians 6:13, 15-17.

230   your
m a r r i a g e
masterpiece

Chapter 10

1. These scenes in heaven are inspired by Jeremiah 2 and 3 and Ezekiel 2 and 16. (Jeremiah was the teenage boy; Ezekiel, the exile in rags.)
2. See Ezekiel 16:8. The phrase "I spread the corner of my garment over you" is literally a declaration of intention to marry.

Chapter 11

1. See Eldredge, John, *The Sacred Romance*, 1997, Thomas Nelson.
2. Jeremiah 3:8.
3. See Matthew 19:1-9 and Mark 10:1-12.
4. Psalm 22:1.
5. Psalm 94:1-3.
6. Isaiah 43:20-22.
7. Exodus 32:9-10.
8. Exodus 32:13 (emphasis added).
9. Dobson, Dr. James C., *Love Must Be Tough*, 1983, Word, pg. 121. (Italics in original.)
10. This is such an important topic that I recommend couples read one or both of the following books: *Guard Your Heart* by Dr. Gary Rosberg, Multnomah Press, 1994; *Loving Your Marriage Enough to Protect It* by Jerry Jenkins, Moody, 1989, 1993. Both books provide practical help for protecting a marriage against affairs and other dangers to marital intimacy.

Chapter 13

1. See Leviticus 20:10—both adulterer and adulteress were to be put to death.
2. Hosea 3:1.
3. Matthew 18:21.

4. Matthew 18:22, alternate translation.
5. Greto, Victor, "Lives Torn Apart," *The Gazette*, Colorado Springs, Colo., Sunday, Nov. 15, 1998, page 1.
6. Matthew 19:9.
7. See 1 Corinthians 7:12-16.
8. *Zondervan NIV Bible Commentary, abridged, volume 2*, 1994, pg. 627.
9. See Esther 2-5, especially 4:12-14 when her Uncle Mordecai reminds her: "Who knows but that you have come to royal position for such a time as this?"
10. See Daniel 3, especially verses 16-18, where the three men tell the king that God is able to rescue them from the blazing furnace. "But even if he does not, we want you to know, O king, that we will not serve your gods or worship the image of gold you have set up."
11. Hebrews 11:39.
12. Matthew 25:21.

Chapter 14
1. See John 6:14-15.
2. Zechariah 9:9.
3. See Luke 15:7 and 15:10.
4. For marriage imagery in the Last Supper, see Vander Laan, Ray, with Markham, Judith, *Echoes of His Presence*, Zondervan, 1996, pp. 18-19.

Chapter 15
1. See Romans 5:12-21.
2. The verse actually reads: "Your attitude should be the same as that of Christ Jesus."
3. See New American Standard Version.
4. Ephesians 5:21-33.

5. Hebrews 12:2 (emphasis added).
6. Mason, Mike, *The Mystery of Marriage*, pg. 152.
7. Ephesians 5:1-2.
8. John 14:15-17.

Chapter 16
1. Isaiah 53:5.
2. Isaiah 53:10.
3. Isaiah 53:11.

Chapter 17
1. Matthew 28:19-20.
2. John 15:7.

Chapter 19
1. Zacharias, Ravi, *Jesus Among Other Gods*, 2000, Word, pg. 85.
2. Matthew 10:39.
3. Romans 12:2.

Study Guide

The problem with writing a book like *Your Marriage Masterpiece* is that so much more could be explored. An author has to make hard choices about what to include, or the text quickly becomes too long. In this book I decided to concentrate on one big idea, then allow readers to meditate on it and consider how it might apply to their own circumstances.

This study guide is intended to help you dig deeper into the rich depths of God's model for marriage. You may want to work through the questions alone, perhaps reflecting on them in a journal. Or you and your spouse may choose to go through this study together. You may even prefer to use this as a framework for a small-group study. Whatever manner you choose, I encourage you to prayerfully ask God to reveal how His marvelous love relationship with you can be reflected in your marriage.

The structure for each of the 12 sessions is as follows:

1. **Points to Ponder:** This will refer to specific content in the book.
2. **Contrasting Pictures:** You are asked to lay the Masterpiece of God's marriage next to what our culture portrays about marriage.
3. **Reflections on the Masterpiece:** You are invited to delve deeper into the Scriptures.
4. **Application of the Masterpiece:** God's marriage should inspire us in our marriages. This section will suggest possible applications.

Do not feel you must answer every question. This is simply a guide, giving you some suggestions of where to go for further reflection and discussion.

Session 1: Whatever Happened to Happily Ever After?

Covering the prologue and chapters 1–3.

Points to Ponder:
1. What was your first reaction to Jim's declaration that he wanted to divorce Bonnie because he was unhappy?
2. What is your reaction to the idea, expressed by Philip Harvey and Dr. David Fromm, that marriage is "an old-fashioned idea"?

Contrasting Pictures:
1. What reasons have you heard among friends or family for getting divorced?
2. If you have any acquaintances who have chosen not to marry (remaining single, cohabiting, or following some other alternative), try to answer these questions: "Why are they making this choice?" "Would you try to change their minds?" "Why or why not?"

Reflections on the Masterpiece:
Read slowly Genesis 1 and 2.
1. If God is truly the Artist, what is your first impression when you look at His creation?
2. Why did God create Adam and Eve in a manner so differently from the rest of the creatures?
3. Why did God make Adam wait before He created Eve? Why show Adam all the other creatures first?

4. Mike Mason writes: "To 'fall in love' actually means…to have a revelation from God." Why do you think he says that?

Application of the Masterpiece:

It has been suggested that in the first marriage Adam and Eve (a) had a three-way relationship among God, husband, and wife, (b) enjoyed a shared adventure, (c) grew together in knowledge, and (d) reflected the image of God as a couple.

Do any of these four things characterize your marriage? Which one(s)?

Try to quantify your answer by rating your marriage in each of these areas (relationship with God, shared adventure, growing in knowledge, and reflecting God's image) on a scale from 1 to 10, with 10 being ideal. What might move your marriage closer to 10?

Session 2: Every Marriage Needs a Hero

Covering chapters 4 and 5.

Points to Ponder:

1. After reading the first five chapters, do you believe Adam and Eve were happy in the Garden of Eden? Why or why not?
2. What do you think attracted the first couple to the tree of the knowledge of good and evil?

Contrasting Pictures:

"Happiness and self-fulfillment were a natural byproduct of marriage as God intended it, but not the primary purpose for marriage." Do you agree with this assessment? Why or why not?

How does that compare with the current cultural thinking about marriage?

Reflections on the Masterpiece:
Read Genesis 3.
1. How could Adam and Eve have helped each other resist the temptation?
2. What were the immediate consequences to the first couple when they disobeyed God's command?
3. What were the long-term consequences to the institution of marriage because of Adam and Eve's disobedience?
4. What evidence do you see today of the Fall as it affects marriages?
5. How much do you think self-centeredness contributed to the fall of Adam and Eve?

Application of the Masterpiece:
"The irony is that self-centeredness often produces the opposite of what we desire.... The more I concentrate on me—on my needs, my desires, my happiness—the less likely I am to find what I want." Prayerfully ask yourself if there is a recent situation when you realized this fact (or a time when you should have and didn't). You may want to write a prayer of confession, admitting where you are selfish in your marriage, and then ask God to change your attitude.

Session 3: A Role Model for Marriage

Based on chapter 5.
Points to Ponder:
Jim, the baseball player, was unhappy being married to Bonnie. What options did Jim have? What are the pros and cons of each option?

Contrasting Pictures:

Noting the prevalence of failed celebrity marriages, we might conclude that "these beautiful people can reveal little to us about true marital happiness." Why do you think so many people look to celebrity marriages as their models?

Reflections on the Masterpiece:

Read Isaiah 54:5-7 and Ezekiel 16:8-14.

1. Why did God get married? What do you think He desires from His marriage?
2. Now read Malachi 2:13-16. God says, "I hate divorce." Why do you think He makes that emphatic statement?
3. Read 2 Corinthians 11:2, Ephesians 5:31-32, and Revelation 19.7-9. The church is described as the bride of Christ. Does that truth affect your own relationship with Christ? If so, how?
4. What does the picture of Christ and His bride, the church, say to you about how God might view your marriage?

Application of the Masterpiece:

1. What is your first reaction when you read, "God got married"?
2. If you could ask one question of God about His marriage, what would it be?

Session 4: God's Marriage Is a Covenant Marriage

Covers chapters 6 and 7.

Points to Ponder:

1. Why do you think God used a familiar human ceremony when making His promise to Abram?
2. What does this say about the way God views promises?

Contrasting Pictures:

Prenuptial agreements begin with the same goal as a covenant: They bind two people together. But is there anything else they have in common? How are they different?

Compare and contrast them for yourself:

Prenuptial Agreement	vs.	*Covenant*
Escape clause		Irrevocable
Witnessed by the state		Witnessed by God
_____		_____
_____		_____
_____		_____
_____		_____

Reflections on the Masterpiece:

Read Isaiah 54:5-10 and Deuteronomy 23:21-23.

1. What do these passages have to say about the way God views a marriage covenant?
2. What do you think most people's understanding of a covenant is today?
3. How does an understanding of the true nature of a covenant change a marriage?

Application of the Masterpiece:

What do you think of the phrase "What doesn't cost much doesn't mean much"? If it is true that price determines value, what price would you affix to your marriage? How many things (small or big) can you think of that boost your relationship's value?

Session 5: God's Marriage Is a Passionate Marriage

Covers chapters 8 and 9.

Points to Ponder:

1. What is your take on the steamy story of love found in the Song of Solomon?
2. Why do you think this story is included in the Bible?

Contrasting Pictures:

1. Our society says two people should stay married as long as they still "love" each other. In other words, loving feelings are the basis for marriage. How is that different from the biblical view?
2. What thoughts or actions constitute adultery? Does it have to include sexual intercourse to be considered adultery? How does God's view differ from the world's or even from what Christians commonly assume?

Reflections on the Masterpiece:

Read Song of Solomon 4—5:1.

1. Why do you think Solomon dwells so long on the physical beauty of his lover?
2. What impact did his deliberate metaphors have on Solomon's bride (v. 16)?
3. What does God seem to be saying to married couples through this passage?

Application of the Masterpiece:

Think back to the first few expressions of love you and your spouse shared with each other.

240   your
m a r r i a g e
masterpiece

1. How has your passion, whether physical or emotional, changed since then?
2. How has your marital commitment affected your passion? Why do you think that is?
3. Do you see value in sustaining romance? What are some ways you want to achieve that?

Session 6: God's Marriage Is a Fighting Marriage

Covers chapters 10 and 11.

Points to Ponder:

1. If you were one of the prophets, how do you think you would have felt knowing the extent of God's jealousy over idolatry?
2. What does God's jealousy tell you about how He views His relationship with His people? Do you think God might have felt trapped like Jim, the baseball player?

Contrasting Pictures:

Our culture teaches us to fight for our own rights or to find a compromise so that both our desires and those of our spouse get equal attention. How is that different from fighting for a marriage, as God did?

Reflections on the Masterpiece:

Read Ezekiel 16:15-63, especially vv. 53-63.

1. What was the source of Israel's unfaithfulness? (see v. 15)
2. Do you think the Israelites understood the covenant they were bound to? Why or why not?
3. Based on the covenant, how did God respond to the threat to His marriage?

4. How does the way that God handled Israel's infidelity demonstrate the right way to fight?

5. Did God adjust His expectations when Israel "cheated" on Him? Are there times when we should adjust our expectations in our relationships?

Application of the Masterpiece:

Your relationship can be conflict-free! All you have to do is always meet your partner's expectations. Sound easy? Of course not! Yet if you can communicate your expectations to your partner openly and honestly, then when a conflict arises, your spouse may be prepared to give special attention to your expectation rather than challenge it.

For this important exercise, try to list your expectations and suggest ways that will help your spouse honor them. Second—but more important—be as honest as you can about your own self-centered expectations and flag them as areas to work on.

Session 7: God's Marriage Is a One-Sided Marriage

Covers chapters 12 and 13.

Points to Ponder:

1. What do you think is the goal of marriage?

2. Can a person in an unhappy marriage still find meaning in the relationship? Why or why not?

3. How did you feel when reading about Joseph's reaction to Georgine's unfaithfulness?

Contrasting Pictures:

What is the common "wisdom" offered today to a person trapped in a one-sided marriage? What justifications are often made for this recommended course of action?

Reflections on the Masterpiece:

Read Hosea 1–3.

1. How closely do you think the details of Hosea's one-sided marriage match the one God endured with Israel?
2. Why do you think that, right after Hosea says God has disowned Israel, he quickly assures them that God will also restore the covenant (1:9-10)?
3. How would you describe God's tone when He promises to win Israel back (2:14-23)?

Application of the Masterpiece:

If your spouse was severely disabled, how would you respond? Or if your spouse became indifferent and unromantic, what would God want you to do?

Session 8: God's Marriage Is a Heroic Marriage

Covers chapters 14 and 15.

Points to Ponder:

Do you think Jesus enjoyed becoming a hero? If yes, why? If not, then why did he do it?

Contrasting Pictures:

Popular entertainment demonstrates that people are obsessed with stories. Touching, dramatic, suspenseful—we live many experiences vicariously in the course of a day.

1. Think of a film or story that portrays self-sacrifice, where the hero puts another person's welfare above his or her own. What was your reaction to this heroic act?
2. If you can, think of another story where the protagonist acted selfishly instead of heroically, compare the two "heroes." Which story was more satisfying?

Reflections on the Masterpiece:

Read Philippians 2:1-11.

1. Paul was writing to the church. But how might this also apply to your marriage? Be specific.
2. What are some ways Jesus "made himself nothing" and took on the form of a servant?
3. Following the example of Christ, how can you serve your spouse?

Read Luke 22:39-46.

4. What is Jesus feeling here?
5. Why is Jesus the ultimate hero?

Application of the Masterpiece:

At the heart of every hero is self-sacrifice. What opportunities do you have to love your mate sacrificially?

Session 9: The Heroic Husband

Covers chapters 14 and 15.

Points to Ponder:

1. Did the pastor whose wife was unfaithful (chapter 15, pages 163-164) have the right to divorce? Why or why not?
2. What were the benefits and liabilities of his decision to fight for his marriage?

Contrasting Pictures:

How does society define a "real man"? Compare that macho image with this book's concept of a hero.

Reflections on the Masterpiece:

Read Ephesians 5:22-33 (especially v. 25) again.

1. How many of these verses talk about marital happiness?

244   your
m a r r i a g e
masterpiece

2. How does Paul say a husband should sacrifice for his wife?

3. What does Jesus' sacrifice tell you about the nature of marital love?

4. What means does the Holy Spirit use to help people understand the "great mystery" concerning Christ and His church?

5. How does Christ's sacrifice for the church put your sacrifice in perspective?

Application of the Masterpiece:

Jesus led by example. Not only did He heroically save us from death, but He also left us a model of perfect love in His deliberate sacrifice. Not many husbands will ever have the chance to die for their wives. Yet there are ways we can show that type of sacrificial love. Look for some specific opportunities in your daily life together.

Session 10: The Heroic Wife

Covers chapters 14 and 15.

Points to Ponder:

1. Shouldn't Linda (chapter 15, pages 168-170) have returned Ron's fire? Or demanded equal consideration for her career? What is your evaluation of her response?

2. "Be imitators of God, therefore..." (Ephesians 5:1). How do you feel knowing you can never attain such a high standard in marriage as the one Paul suggests?

Contrasting Pictures:

In our culture, submission and servanthood usually mean playing an inferior role and being less valued than someone in a leadership position. How does this match or differ from the Bible's view?

Reflections on the Masterpiece:
Read Genesis 2:18-24 again. Also Ephesians 5:22-33.
1. What are the roles given for wives in these verses?
2. How does the idea of self-sacrifice for wives differ from that of husbands?
3. How do you see this ideal playing out in your sacrifices for your husband?

Application of the Masterpiece:
Think of a specific instance when you can sacrifice for your husband. Be creative.

Session 11: Return to Eden

Covers chapters 16 and 17.

Points to Ponder:
1. What is required to make marriage a three-way relationship?
2. Think of a couple you know who seem to be pursuing an adventure together. How does that help their marriage?

Contrasting Pictures:
Why do most people get married? What adventure or shared purpose (if any) seems to underlie the marriages you observe around you?

Reflections on the Masterpiece:
Read Genesis 12:1-9.
1. What do you think Abram and Sarai felt when God told Abram to "leave your country, your people and your father's household and go to the land I will show you"?
2. Describe in your own words the joint adventure that God was setting before Abram and his wife.

Read Galatians 5:16-26.

3. How does the Holy Spirit help marriages "return to Eden"?

Application of the Masterpiece:
1. Talk as a couple about the adventure you've been on with God and where you think it's heading. Then discuss your goals and purposes. What does God want to accomplish through you together?
2. For the next week, spend a few minutes each day in prayer together about your goals.

Session 12: Is There Happiness in Our Future?

Covers chapters 18 and 19.

Points to Ponder:
1. Have you experienced a transcendent moment with your partner as Al and Jo did? If so, how did it affect you and your relationship?
2. What are some ways in which you could expand or capitalize on that moment?

Contrasting Pictures:

What value does the world place on happiness in marriage? How important is it to you? Is your happiness dependent on your spouse's intellectual or physical attractiveness? What if that attraction fades over time?

Reflections on the Masterpiece:

Read Revelation 19:6-9.
1. What significance does this coming marriage have for your own relationship now?

Read Revelation 21:1-7.

2. What does John's description promise to believers?

3. How does this hope of things to come help you deal with marital troubles here and now?

Application of the Masterpiece:

1. What are some ways you've noticed yourself thinking differently about marriage in general, or your marriage in particular, after viewing God's Masterpiece?

2. Based on God's picture of marriage, what are three things you can do in the next month to cause your marriage to reflect God's image?

Bibliography

There are so many books about marriage. Over the years I have read many, and in preparation to write this book, I looked at many more. Still, I've read only a fraction of what is available to the couple who want to build a strong marriage. This bibliography is not exhaustive but rather reflects my own journey. Not all of the titles are explicitly about marriage, but all touch on the subject in some way. It is my hope that within this list readers will find tools to help them develop their marriage relationships and let God make their marriages into reflections of His Masterpiece.

Allender, Dan B., and Longman, Tremper. *Intimate Allies.* Wheaton, Ill.: Tyndale House Publishers, 1995. This is one of the best explorations of the biblical meaning of marriage.

Anderson, Neil T., and Charles Mylander. *The Christ-Centered Marriage: Discovering and Enjoying Your Freedom in Christ Together.* Ventura, Calif.: Regal Books, 1996. Neil Anderson applies his "Steps to Freedom in Christ" to marriage.

Arp, David and Claudia. *The Second Half of Marriage.* Grand Rapids, Mich.: Zondervan Publishing House, 1996. The dynamics of marriage change as we grow older, especially when the children leave home. This resource helps couples create a vision for the rest of their life together.

Brokaw, Tom. *The Greatest Generation.* New York: Random House, 1998. I was particularly moved by the section on love, marriage, and commitment.

Capon, Robert Farrar. *Bed and Board: Plain Talk About Marriage.*
New York: Simon and Schuster, 1965. This was one of the
first books I read about marriage. It contains solid biblical
advice.

Chapell, Bryan. *Each for the Other: Marriage As It's Meant to Be.*
Grand Rapids, Mich.: Baker Books, 1998. A strong examination of the meaning of marriage as revealed in Scripture.

Colson, Charles, and Nancy Pearcey. *How Now Shall We Live?*
Carol Stream, Ill.: Tyndale House, 1999. Colson's challenge
to articulate a Christian worldview of marriage and family
helped inspire *Your Marriage Masterpiece.*

Crosby, Robert and Pamela. *Conversation Starters for Couples.* Colorado Springs, Colo.: Focus on the Family, 1996. It seems like
you can't stop talking before you're married. But after you say "I
do," conversation often becomes more difficult. This handy
little volume helps couples keep the communication lines open.

Dobson, Dr. James C. *Love for a Lifetime.* Portland, Ore.: Multnomah Press, 1987.

___. *Love Must Be Tough.* Waco, Texas: Word, 1983.

___. *Straight Talk to Men and Their Wives.* Dallas, Texas: Word, 1984.

___. *What Wives Wish Their Husbands Knew About Women.*
Wheaton, Ill.: Living Books, 1975.

Every newlywed couple should read *Love for a Lifetime* and
Straight Talk to Men and Their Wives, and every husband should
be required to read *What Wives Wish Their Husbands Knew
About Women.* For those couples who are struggling and con-
templating divorce, *Love Must Be Tough* deals with the core
issues.

Faludi, Susan. *Stiffed: The Betrayal of the American Man.* New
York: William Morrow and Company, 1999. A powerful examination of what has happened to men in our culture.

Farrar, Steve. *If I'm Not Tarzan and My Wife Isn't Jane, Then What Are We Doing in the Jungle?* Portland, Ore.: Multnomah Press, 1991. I have a great respect for Steve and his uncompromising challenge to men to be what God meant them to be. This book helps couples navigate through the materialism of our culture.

Gilder, George. *Men and Marriage.* Gretna, La.: Pelican Publishing Company, 1986. A powerful examination of what is wrong with marriage today.

Gottman, John, Ph.D. *Why Marriages Succeed or Fail...and How You Can Make Yours Last.* New York: Simon and Schuster, 1994. Psychologist John Gottman reveals the results of 20-plus years of research into what makes a marriage last.

Grant, Dave. *The Great Lover's Manifesto.* Eugene, Ore.: Harvest House Publishers, 1986. A wonderful little book that explores what love is and what love does.

Hart, Archibald D., Catherine Hart Weber, and Debra L. Taylor. *Secrets of Eve: Understanding the Mystery of Female Sexuality.* Nashville, Tenn.: Word Publishing, 1998. A survey of more than 2,000 women in Christian churches. Shows how Christian women feel about sex and sexuality.

Hillerstrom, P. Roger. *Intimate Deception: Escaping the Trap of Sexual Impurity.* Portland, Ore.: Multnomah Press, 1989. It's a shame this book is out of print, for it is one of the best statements I've seen about God's intention for sex and why it is intended only for marriage.

Holt, Betsy, and Mike Yorkey. *Always: Inspiring Stories to Encourage Your Marriage.* Carol Stream, Ill.: Tyndale House Publishers, 1999. Eight powerful stories that demonstrate how every marriage can go the distance, regardless of the trials it endures. Contains commentary by Gary Smalley.

Jenkins, Jerry. *Still the One: Tender Thoughts from a Loving Spouse.* Colorado Springs, Colo.: Focus on the Family, 1995. A wonderful little gift book to celebrate marriage.

___. *Loving Your Marriage Enough to Protect It.* Chicago: Moody, 1989., 1993. This was originally published under the title of *Hedges.* I believe every couple needs to read this book for the very practical help it provides in protecting their marriage.

LaHaye, Tim and Beverly. *The Act of Marriage: The Beauty of Sexual Love.* Grand Rapids, Mich.: Zondervan Publishing House, 1976. A classic on marital intimacy.

Lepine, Bob. *The Christian Husband: God's Vision for Loving and Caring for Your Wife.* Ann Arbor, Mich.: Vine Books, 1999. Bob gets down to the nitty-gritty of what it means for a husband to love his wife sacrificially.

Mason, Mike. *The Mystery of Marriage.* Portland, Ore.: Multnomah Press, 1985. This is my personal favorite—a book that explores the wonder of marriage and reveals the masterpiece of God's creation.

McCartney, Bill and Lyndi, and Connie Neal. *Sold Out Two-Gether: A Couples Workbook.* Nashville, Tenn.: Word Publishing, 1999. A tool for couples to work through together.

McQuilkin, Robertson. *A Promise Kept: The Story of an Unforgettable Love.* Carol Stream, Ill.: Tyndale House Publishers, 1998. This is the story of McQuilkin's love for his wife as she suffered from Alzheimer's. For me, this is one of the most moving examples of heroic love.

Miller, Calvin. *If This Be Love: The Journey of Two People Toward Each Other in Love and Marriage.* San Francisco, Calif.: Harper and Row Publishers, 1984. A beautifully written love story.

Nieder, John and Teri. *The Marriage Maker: The Holy Spirit and the Hidden Power of Becoming One.* Eugene, Ore.: Harvest House

Publishers, 1996. This is the only book I've found that examines the role of the Holy Spirit in marriage.

Parrott, Drs. Les and Leslie. *When Bad things Happen to Good Marriages.* Grand Rapids, Mich.: Zondervan Publishing House, 2001. Les and Leslie Parrott have developed some wonderful resources for couples. This book provides a much-needed message. Regardless of how good our marriage is, sooner or later life will throw us some tough times. The Parrotts coach couples in how to let those times draw them closer together rather than pulling them apart.

Piper, John. *Desiring God: Meditations of a Christian Hedonist.* Portland, Ore.: Multnomah Press, 1986. I highly recommend chapter eight, "Marriage: A Matrix for Christian Hedonism."

Rainey, Dennis. *One Home at a Time.* Colorado Springs, Colo.: Focus on the Family, 1997. Dennis' examination of the covenant in marriage—chapter five—is outstanding. It is the centerpiece of a call for a family reformation in America.

___. *We Still Do.* Nashville, Tenn.: Thomas Nelson Publishers, 2001.

___. *Starting Your Marriage Right.* Nashville, Tenn.: Thomas Nelson Publishers, 2000.

___. *Building Your Mate's Self-Esteem.* Ventura, Calif.: Gospel Light, 1990, 1997.

Dennis is cofounder and executive director of FamilyLife, a division of Campus Crusade for Christ. I would encourage every couple to attend a FamilyLife marriage conference. Also consider participating in a FamilyLife HomeBuilders study for couples. For more information on a conference near you, or a list of the HomeBuilders studies, contact FamilyLife, P.O. Box 23840, Little Rock, AR 72221-3840, or call 1-800-FL-TODAY, or visit www.familylife.com.

Rainey, Dennis and Barbara. *Moments Together for Couples*. Ventura, Calif.: Regal Books, 1995. The best devotional I know of for couples.

Robinson, Constance. *Passion and Marriage*. London: S.P.C.K., 1965. A fascinating little gem I found in my parents' library.

Rosberg, Dr. Gary. *Dr. Rosberg's Do-It-Yourself Relationship Mender: A Remarkable Remedy for Unresolved Conflict*. Colorado Springs, Colo.: Focus on the Family, 1992, 1995. This is an excellent tool for helping couples resolve conflict.

___. *Guard Your Heart*. Sisters, Ore.: Multnomah Books, 1994. This is a must for men who need help in protecting their moral character. Copies may be ordered from America's Family Coaches, 2540 106th St., Suite 101, Urbandale, IA 50322.

Smalley, Gary. *Keys to Loving Relationships*. This is a video series that has helped literally millions of couples around the world. For information on how to order this resource, contact the Smalley Relationship Center, 1482 Lakeshore Drive, Branson, MO 65616, or call 1-800-848-6329.

___. *Making Love Last Forever*. Dallas, Texas: Word Publishing, 1996. Classic material containing Gary's proven advice and techniques.

Smalley, Gary and Norma. *It Takes Two to Tango: More than 250 Secrets to Communication, Romance and Intimacy in Marriage*. Colorado Springs, Colo.: Focus on the Family, 1997. An excellent gift book that provides many of Gary's best insights on what makes a successful marriage.

Smalley, Gary, with Al Janssen. *Joy That Lasts*, Grand Rapids, Mich.: Zondervan Publishing House, 2000. This is a revised edition of a book Gary and I wrote together in 1986. It chronicles Gary's spiritual journey that led to his discovery of five principles that transformed his life and his marriage.

Smalley, Gary, and John Trent, Ph.D. *The Language of Love: A Powerful Way to Maximize Insight, Intimacy, and Understanding.* Pomona, Calif.: Focus on the Family, 1988.
___. *The Two Sides of Love.* Pomona, Calif.: Focus on the Family, 1990.
___. *The Hidden Value of a Man: The Incredible Impact of a Man on His Family.* Colorado Springs, Colo.: Focus on the Family, 1992, 1994.
Snyder, Chuck. *Men: Some Assembly Required: A Woman's Guide to Understanding Her Man.* Wheaton, Ill.: Living Books, 1995, 2001. Chuck relaxes readers with his winsome humor, but women will get very helpful insight into how men think.
Snyder, Chuck and Barb. *Incompatibility: Grounds for a Great Marriage.* Phoenix, Ariz.: Questar Publishers, 1988. This classic has been reissued several times. When you read this, you will recognize my tribute to Chuck and Barb in chapter 18.
Sproul, R. C. *The Intimate Marriage: A Practical Guide to Building a Great Marriage.* Wheaton, Ill.: Living Books, 1975, 1986. A good overview of what Scripture says about marriage.
Stanley, Scott. *The Heart of Commitment: Compelling Research that Reveals the Secrets of a Lifelong, Intimate Marriage.* Nashville, Tenn.: Thomas Nelson Publishers, 1998. I particularly appreciate Dr. Stanley's encouragement to couples to develop a shared vision.
Stanley, Scott, Daniel Trathen, Savanna McCain, and Milt Bryan. *A Lasting Promise: A Christian Guide to Fighting for Your Marriage.* San Francisco, Calif.: Jossey-Bass Publishers, 1998. This is a Christian adaptation of the classic book *Fighting for Your Marriage* by Howard Markman, Scott Stanley, and Susan L. Blumberg, which presents the well-established PREP approach.

Stanton, Glenn T. *Why Marriage Matters: Reasons to Believe in Marriage in Postmodern Society.* Colorado Springs, Colo.: Piñon Press, 1997. Glenn provides the research that shows why commitment to the institution of marriage is in the best interests of society.

Vanauken, Sheldon. *A Severe Mercy.* San Francisco: Harper and Row Publishers, 1977. Jo and I read this book during the first year of our marriage. It is the best story I've found that reveals the heart of true romance. Includes 18 letters from C. S. Lewis.

Waite, Linda J., and Maggie Gallagher. *The Case for Marriage: Why Married People Are Happier, Healthier, and Better Off Financially.* New York: Doubleday, 2000. Here at last are the studies and statistics showing the long-term benefits of marriage on individuals and society.

Wallerstein, Judith S., and Sandra Blakeslee. *The Good Marriage: How and Why Love Lasts.* New York: Warner Books, 1995. This is a sociological study of what makes a good marriage.

Wallerstein, Judith S., Julia M. Lewis, and Sandra Blakeslee. *The Unexpected Legacy of Divorce: A 25-Year Landmark Study.* New York: Hyperion, 2000. This is a superb study on the effects of divorce on adult children.

Whitehead, Barbara Dafoe. *The Divorce Culture: Rethinking Our Commitments to Marriage and Family.* New York: Vintage Books, 1996. This book develops the theme Whitehead introduced in her monumental article for *Atlantic Monthly,* "Dan Quayle Was Right." She examines the origins and consequences of divorce.

FOCUS ON THE FAMILY®

Welcome to the family!

Whether you purchased this book, borrowed it, or received it as a gift, we're glad you're reading it. It's just one of the many helpful, encouraging, and biblically based resources produced by Focus on the Family for people in all stages of life.

Focus began in 1977 with the vision of one man, Dr. James Dobson, a licensed psychologist and author of numerous best-selling books on marriage, parenting, and family. Alarmed by the societal, political, and economic pressures that were threatening the existence of the American family, Dr. Dobson founded Focus on the Family with one employee and a once-a-week radio broadcast aired on 36 stations.

Now an international organization reaching millions of people daily, Focus on the Family is dedicated to preserving values and strengthening and encouraging families through the life-changing message of Jesus Christ.

Focus on the Family Magazines

These faith-building, character-developing publications address the interests, issues, concerns, and challenges faced by every member of your family from preschool through the senior years.

| Focus on the Family **Citizen®** U.S. news issues | Focus on the Family **Clubhouse Jr.™** Ages 4 to 8 | Focus on the Family **Clubhouse™** Ages 8 to 12 | **Breakaway®** Teen guys | **Brio®** Teen girls 12 to 16 | **Brio & Beyond®** Teen girls 16 to 19 | **Plugged In®** Reviews movies, music, TV |

FOR MORE INFORMATION

 Online:
Log on to www.family.org
In Canada, log on to www.focusonthefamily.ca

 Phone:
Call toll free: (800) A-FAMILY (232-6459)
In Canada, call toll free: (800) 661-9800

BP06XFM

Make the most of your relationships with resources from Focus on the Family®!

From dating and engagement to the wedding and beyond, we're here to help your marriage thrive.

First Comes Love, Then What?
Myths about finding Mr. or Mrs. Right are held to be true by too many men and women searching for that one-in-a-million match. It's time for a reality check. Filled with real-life examples and solid principles, this book will help both men and women learn to use their heads before losing their hearts. Paperback F00727B

Countdown for Couples
Research and common sense indicate that engaged couples will have stronger, more successful marriages if they participate in premarital counseling. Yet with all the planning that goes into a wedding, this important preparation can often be overlooked. *Countdown for Couples* delivers insight in an easy-to-use format and tackles important questions such as: *Are you ready for a lifelong commitment? What should you expect?* And more! Paperback F00863B

The Savvy Bride's Answer Guide
Your maid of honor might not tell you, but the price of your wedding dress isn't the only thing that may shock you about wedded bliss. During the first year of marriage, you're likely to face all kinds of surprises—from your in-laws' strange traditions to your groom's annoying tendencies. This friendly resource will smooth the road whether you've been engaged for 10 minutes or married for 10 months. Paperback F00857B

The Smart Groom's Answer Guide
Launching your lifetime love? Getting biblical answers is the smart thing to do! This book provides down-to-earth advice from a team of professional Focus on the Family counselors. You'll get the real story on questions like *What does it mean to be a husband? Why does she want to talk all the time?* And more! Ask now—or forever hold your peace! Paperback F00856B

![marriage]

Focus on the Family's Complete Guide to the First Five Years of Marriage

Building and maintaining a good marriage isn't easy, but the rewards are priceless. Focus on the Family counselors present practical, biblical answers to 112 questions commonly asked by recently married spouses. This handy reference empowers couples for a lifetime partnership filled with genuine love and joy.
Hardcover F00271B

Blueprints for a Solid Marriage

A marriage, like a house, requires time, effort, and regular maintenance. Get immediate practical assistance in this unique do-it-yourself guide to a better marriage. This practical hardcover helps time-strapped couples assess and enhance their relationships with engaging stories and a detailed plan.
Hardcover F00233B

The Language of Love: How to Be Instantly Understood by Those You Love

Words have incredible meaning, especially when they say what you mean. Make the most of your messages by learning *The Language of Love*. It shows how "emotional word pictures" can infuse understanding and intimacy into *all* of your relationships.
Paperback F00227B

Your Marriage Masterpiece

This thoughtful, creative book takes a fresh appraisal of the exquisite design God has for a man and woman. Explaining the reasons why this union is meant to last a lifetime, it also shows how God's relationship with humanity is the model for marriage.
Paperback BL550

The Way to Love Your Wife

With this book, noted sex therapists Clifford and Joyce Penner help husbands keep the passion going and take their marriage to a level that's better than they ever imagined. They cover everything from building desire and enjoying guilt-free sex to getting past sexual problems.
Paperback F00705B